The
ADVERTISER'S ALPHABET

An Entrepreneur's Guide to Business Growth and Brand Development

Andrew Hindle

CEO of Stacked Deck, a Software Development Company that Specializes in Advertising

Copyright © 2024 Andrew Hindle
All rights reserved
First Edition

Fulton Books
Meadville, PA

Published by Fulton Books 2024

This book or any portion thereof may not be reproduced or used in any manner whatsoever without the express written permission of the publisher except for the use of brief quotations in a book review or as a reference in publications.

ISBN 979-8-88505-808-7 (paperback)
ISBN 979-8-88505-809-4 (digital)

Printed in the United States of America

Contents

Acknowledgments v
Introduction vii
Accommodate 1
Brand 5
Content 12
Differentiate 16
Ego 20
Fluctuation 24
Gather 28
Habit 33
Illuminate 36
Judgment 39
    The Bad News 39
    The Good News 40
Keep 42
Luck 45
Messaging 47
No 51
Oath 54
Product 57
Quotable 61
Referrals 64
Story 67
Truth 70
Umbrella 74
Value 79
Wait 83
X: Variable 87
You 93
Zero 97
A Little Extra 101

Acknowledgments

I want to thank a few outstanding people and business owners for making my work possible.

- Frank Hogan, Jen Smith, and Mark Smith, Founders and Owners of Hogan Construction
- Dustin and Ellis Olde of Automotive Evolution
- Staci Danford, CEO and founder of The Grateful Brain and a TEDx speaker

Introduction

I believe that authors in different industries write books for various reasons, whether it's authentic help, financial gain, or personal development; these days, it's hard to understand a writer's, politician's, or even your parents' motives for saying, writing, or doing something. This is why (you may have heard) "when you want something done right, do it yourself." In my case, I am writing with the hope of waking people up so that they can take action for themselves in regard to their businesses and careers. I chose business owners as the target audience for this book because they have *gathered* (see Gather) and garnered the biggest following and have the most well-known reputation, and they tend to have money in their bank account (a means for taking action on behalf of a cause greater than themselves). *You are the protagonist in your Story, so what do You want to be remembered for?*

I never intended to start my own company; it's a grind, day after day, not to mention handling the roller coaster of emotions from clients and employees that come with any leadership role, but someone must do it, and that someone needs to be you (see You).

This book examines problems relating to business and recommends techniques and best practices for personal leadership development and business growth. These best practices can also be applied to your daily life and help smooth out those speed bumps that we all endure.

The advertising industry's reputation has been tarnished, its faults and errors have been disseminated throughout the business world and not for lack of a good reason. There is no standard (i.e., CPA Certification, BAR exam or pilot's license) required to advertise a business and this has led to a wild, wild west advertising environment perceived by most business owners, including myself. The goal of this book is in part to combat the infamous opinions about the advertising industry with simple techniques and best practices.

If *you* find that these principles work well for you, I ask that you share them by evocating and enacting these principles in your daily lives—be the change you want to see.

Accommodate

Make it easy to do business with you and your clients. Accommodate the customer's preferences before they even know they have them. Making it seamless to do business reduces exit opportunities before meaningful engagement, whether that be purchasing a product or ad interaction.

When you walk into a Chick-fil-A (politics aside), yes, you're going for the chicken, but what keeps their following so strong is the five-star customer experience they provide. It's obvious that they not only take care of their customers but also their employees. Chick-fil-A knows how to brand a business through accommodation of its employees and customers.

So how does accommodation affect me? What if I own an online business? How would I possibly provide the same experience as a company like Chick-fil-A? The answer is simple: provide value to the client or potential client before asking them to spend any money on your product or service.

Market saturation has left us all in a buyer's market, meaning the buyer has all the power. If they don't like one (little thing) about you or your business, you're done, and they're onto the next person (your competitor). *They could even leave you a bad review along the way.* Accommodate your clients with everything in your arsenal. Open the door for your clients, hand them a bottle of water, and ask them how they're doing; make them feel like they've been noticed and will be remembered so that you can too. Make your customers feel as if they are the most important person in the world when they enter your store or experience your services.

When you provide a five-star experience, you create an association of accommodation to the company's brand. Word travels fastest outside of work, so it's what you do with your employees while they're at work that matters when scaling a brand. Think globally, work locally. Don't try and fix problems that are out of your reach or control; rather, focus on what's in front of you; serve the customers you have—make them want to tell their friends about you, and delight them (see Referrals). So many times, I've heard clients ask me, "How do I get rid of this bad review You don't get rid of the bad review; you go fix the problem with the person who wrote the review and treat them with respect; that's the best thing you can do for yourself.

Be proactive in knowing how a customer wants to be provided with choices, and use the language that resonates with them. Make interaction easy.

If you're not seeing the result you expected, spend time to research test for what is actually going on. For example, a client wanted to know why one of their pages wasn't seeing a lot of use. Tracking how web visitors interacted with their page allowed us to see the link to the page isn't in the optimal spot to get noticed and wasn't offered a visitor to use it.

Here's what you need to do:

1. Greet them by name.
2. Offer them a sample upon entering your store or a gift branded with your company's logo. A great example of this is liquor stores that offer simple bottle openers with their logo. Not only are you delighting customers with a free gift but you're accommodating them by making it simple to consume your products.
3. Ask them about something specific relating to their personal lives to show that you care about them as an individual: How is their day going? How are their pets? How have they been fairing during the current shared experience (weather, holiday, etc.)?
4. Send thank you cards to customers after they purchase from you.
5. Offer discounts to repeat customers or a loyalty program for customers to earn points toward a free service or gift.

6. Create a customer journey and touchpoints that rewards customers who show up on time to appointments. Utilize their preferred communication tool to send reminders and thank you. This approach has the added benefit of collecting customer contact information.

Questions to Consider:

- *What will it cost me to correctly accommodate my clients, customers, and employees on a monthly basis? Do I have room for it in my budget? If not, make room in that budget!*
- *Do I need to accommodate my clients, customers, and employees if _____?*

For example, let's say you're a digital bookkeeper and you don't have the need for a brick-and-mortar office. The answer is *yes*; you need to accommodate them with a five-star customer experience as well as send something like a thank you card at the end of the calendar or fiscal year to show your appreciation. Something small like this goes a long way in client retention.

Troubleshooting

- If a client or customer is difficult to work with, ask them what you can do to make their experience better with you and your business.
- If they decide to cancel services altogether, ask them if they will take your exit survey or would be willing to take part in an exit interview—similar to if you were losing an employee.
- Ask your employees or existing clients what would make your office or business a better experience for everyone. You'd be surprised at what you can learn simply by asking.
- If you don't know what you should be doing to better accommodate your employees, clients, and customers

because of the specific nature of your work, try reaching out to colleagues in your service industry for advice. I highly recommend having a mother or father figure in your line of business so that you can ask questions pertaining to your business.

Story

Accommodation is what keeps me in business. If I don't make money for a client during that billing period, I move their payment out. If they're having a grand opening of a new location, I fly out to help them with the launch. I work in advertising, which means I work in digital advertising, which implies that I know how to use a computer. This means that if a client is paying me a monthly retainer, it is implied and expected that I fix their computer issues within reasonable relevancy to match their advertising and growth goals. I'm not above any type of work, nor should I be. This should apply to your industry in a way that matches your services.

Be willing to take the extra step for your clients, customers, and employees, and they'll be willing to take the extra step for you when the time comes.

Brand

A brand is an idea worth dying for, so make sure you believe in the idea you're selling to the world. Branding is a large term that can be defined and executed in many ways, but the easiest way to think about it is that you are deciding on a messaging strategy or desired perception for your business. The process for branding a Fortune 500 company and a small business is exactly the same. The first thing to do when branding is finding your target audience and narrowing it down to a perspective that can be understood by everyone in your company. When advertising, don't think about selling to a group of people; rather, think of selling to a single, specific person. Talk to them like you're face to face with them; laser target your audience—not everyone will like you, so don't worry about the people who dislike your campaign; rather, focus on the people who do react positively to your messaging. In fact, the more focused and targeted your campaign is, the more effective it will become with the target audience, but the more divisive or non-applicable it will become to others.

    Not every campaign needs this hyper-focus broad awareness campaigns, but as consumers get deeper into the funnel, it is really important to tighten this. But there is potential for blowback from the unintended public if the campaign is socially-charged (think of recent Nike campaigns or even Chick-fil-A campaigns); the unintended public may view it as tone-deaf, not inclusive enough, alienating, or infuriating, but it was never intended for them anyway (though you do need to consider their power to recognize its applicability to someone else in their lives and spread it to them if the message is acceptable to them). As you narrow down your audience, you will start to see that the people you are targeting are almost always giving you positive reactions; therefore, you've created an audience that can yield infinite amounts of revenue depending on your product or service.

Developing a brand and positioning yourself within your competitive marketplace is paramount to the success of your company, so these two things should be among the first you do. While branding, you also need to develop and decide upon a few things: your target audience profile, your brand's tone of voice, and perceived following or club. A great voice for a company will be representative of the business owner and their employees; be true to who you are and what you stand for. The perceived following stands for what you want people to think of your business's customers as. This can be confusing, so consider Apple products; they're designed so that no instruction manual is needed to use the product; therefore, their perceived following would be people who aren't tech-savvy or the everyday user.

Branding yourself and your company is the building blocks of a business worth buying from. So you need to have a messaging strategy that is so cleanly packaged that *when you hire someone, you can hand them a one-page document that sums up your entire brand.* A messaging strategy can be defined as how you portray yourself to the audience—what types of adjectives do you use to describe your business? Is your business meant to be seen as *clean and professional*, or is it *playful and helpful?* Make sure that you choose your words carefully in correspondence with your power base or existing clients and target audience. Cleanly packaging your product for sale is extremely important. This includes creating a singular desired outcome that you're looking for; for example, you want to sell more widgets, so creating an offer around your widgets that corresponds to the needs of your audience is step one.

After you've created the offer, you need to create the customer journey and/or sales process for what the client or customer experiences from first point of contact with your business to becoming a repeat customer. What emails do they get after making a purchase? Do you have high-ticket services that an email campaign could actually hurt your appearance? Does your offer create unwanted sales traffic that actually slows your business down? Is the offer priced too high, and you're not seeing any traffic?

These are all things to consider when cleanly packaging your product. After taking into consideration as many data points as possible for your brand, you are ready to put them into a one-page document (for internal use only) that you can hang on your wall for your employees as a reminder of the bigger picture for your business. The next thing you'll want to do is implement the branding strategy. Rather than telling everyone about the strategy, the first thing you need to do is get all your employees on the same page about what your business does, what it stands for, why you do what you do, and how it should be spoken to the outside world. Everyone needs to be in agreement on this; otherwise, you can create dissociation from the brand (different employees saying different things about your products and services).

The single thing that makes some brands successful and followable is not in your color scheme, slogan, or secret sauce; it's the fact that they have branded internally (within their company, among their employees) before going public with it. Once you do this, you can rest easy, knowing that all your employees can proudly embody and represent your company, even when they're not wearing your uniform (at work or on the clock).

A key misstep here is that some people think these are independent, or at least only loosely related to each other and develop independently of each other (not sure if I'm explaining this correctly). But the tone of voice and perceived following have to spring from the target audience profile. A lot of entrepreneurs have an idea of what target audience they want to focus on and then think that the brand's tone of voice should reflect them or sound like the people around them who are supportive of their efforts. You have to speak to your target audience in their language, and if that isn't a natural voice for you, then you need to hire someone who speaks that language fluently.

Here's what you need to do:

1. Define your target audience using existing customer data (what has worked for you in the past, or what segment

of your audience have you not tapped into yet that may become a valuable and loyal part of your consumer base).
   a. Demographics
      i. How old are your average customers?
      ii. What is the common geographic location of your customers?
      iii. Are your customers mostly men or women?
   b. Psychographics
      i. What are your customers' behaviors and interests?
      ii. What motivates your customer to consume within your product category?
      iii. What other people do your customers engage with, and what activities are they involved in?

2. Determine where your brand is positioned within your competitive landscape.
   a. Who are your competitors?
   b. How does their pricing compare to yours?
   c. What does their target audience look like compared to yours?
   d. Is your brand new to the product category, a leader in the product category?
   e. How does your target customer define the product category?

3. Define your messaging strategy.
   a. What are adjectives to describe your business?
   b. A company doesn't have a personality—the people do, so make sure the people are in agreement with what you want to be seen as
   c. Make sure your messaging is geared toward your desired outcome (does it increase revenue, spread awareness, emotionally connect, establish or rein-

THE ADVERTISER'S ALPHABET

force a personality, differentiate your product from competitors, etc.)

4. Implement the strategy internally before implementing it to your audience.
    a. Make sure your employees understand that you are putting out a clear message to an identified target audience.
    b. Make sure that all digital assets (website, Facebook, Instagram, business pages, etc.) are in alignment with your messaging strategy.

5. Ask the audience—ask your customers—and get a reading on what's going on; don't be afraid to ask your clients what they think of you. Some will be eager to tell you, and others will run and hide after you ask, but you still need to do it.
    a. This one seems obvious because you talk to your employees every day, right? If you don't, you should. Don't make an ordeal out of it, but make sure that you and your employees are on the same page about the direction of the business.
    b. There's always room for improvement, so even if you're sittin' pretty and you don't have a care in the world, start thinking about how you can give back to your community that helped grow your business. Create a positive impact in your community; givers gain.

Questions to Consider:

- *How do people currently perceive my brand?*
    - You can find this out by asking current or previous clients or customers; even try asking your employees.

- *How do people want to reach my brand?*
  - Again, this is something you'll want to ask your constituents about.
- *How do my employees currently perceive my brand?*
  - Ask them, get on the same page, then execute as a team.
- *How can I improve my existing brand?*
  - For this, you'll want to hire an expert to do an audit of your brand's current standing throughout the existing channels you're using.

Troubleshooting

- Avoid using different color schemes across multiple pages and platforms.
- Avoid using different tones of voice in the writing of your social media content; this is what your users will think of you.
- Watch out for employees who blatantly disagree with your *messaging*; help them find a job that is the right fit for them rather than trying to mold them into something they're not; this can get you killed.

Story

It doesn't matter what the industry is or what you're selling; your *brand* needs to be an idea worth dying for (or at least worth going to battle for). The most important factor when deciding on a *brand* is that you're solving a problem, you're filling a need, or you're starting a cause worth following. In my company's case, the problem that needed solving was that I was in a saturated industry where none of my competitors seemed to treat my clients with respect, so I solved the problem, and money followed.

THE ADVERTISER'S ALPHABET

When I was creating a campaign for Charles Schwab, understanding the *brand* (before conducting research) was paramount to the success of the campaign. It was also important to show the client (VP of marketing) that we knew what we were talking about and that our suggestions were relevant to their company. If we had assumed that they were following the same brand attributes as, for example, Merril Lynch, then that could've killed our campaign before it even left the gates, so make sure to do the front-end work required for your client beforehand; it shows that you care and are willing to go the extra mile to make them happy *and* make them money.

Content

Content marketing should be a part of every marketing strategy regardless of what industry you're in. I spent a lot of time deliberating over whether or not the "Q" in this book should be for "quotable" or "quality" because there is (literally) nothing that beats quality content. If you're trying to convince someone who has never heard of your business to become a paying customer and the photos on your website are pixelated, outdated, and out of place, or if your website is not intuitively mobile-friendly, the potential customer's perception of your business will now be worse than it would be if they had never heard of it; they've created a negative association with your business and brand (whether they realize it or not), and they're onto the next business who fits their needs.

The customer's perception is your reality, so it's really important to make sure that you do everything in your power to make the first impression (digital presence) of your business a good one because these days, word travels faster than ever, and it's not slowing down. All it takes is one person to see one poorly made piece of content to create a dissociation with your brand.

So instead of thinking of your content creation (photographer/videographer/website designer) as an annoying expense, think of it as an opportune investment for your business. Once you have a beautiful overview video and jaw-dropping photos of your business, you now have digitals assets that can and will make you *a lot* of money if used correctly.

Another thing to note about content is that it should be posted at the same time every week; otherwise, the social media algorithms will ding you for lack of consistency and reliability. The goal of social media is to provide users with a high-quality, relevant experience so that they keep returning. If you have good content, social media platforms will love you.

THE ADVERTISER'S ALPHABET

Here's what you need to do:

1. You need to have an overview video of your business.

    It doesn't matter if you're brick-and-mortar or strictly online sales, an overview video gives people that have never met you, seen your business or your website, don't know anything about you or your business a taste of what to expect from working with you and your team.

2. Make sure you create a schedule for your social media posts.

    Even if it's once every two weeks, make sure you're doing it around the same day and time each time you post; the social media algorithms are looking for consistency and reliability, so you can always increase the frequency of how often you post, but decreasing the frequency will tell Facebook, Google, YouTube, etc., that your business is in a decline.

3. Put as much production quality into your content as possible because the customer's perception is your reality. If they see content that looks like it was made last minute on a 2008 flip phone, then they're going to think that is the quality of work you do.

Questions to Consider:

- *What type of content am I supposed to make for my business? I don't know where to begin.*
    - Niche, narrow, and specific topics are always best because you want to put out as much information as possible, and you don't want to have overlapping content.
        - For example, if you're a chiropractor, put out a video once a week on a simple stretch

or exercise you can do to improve your overall health and wellness.

- *How often should I be putting out content for my business?*
    - Once per week is the sweet spot from my experience, but you can post twice a week if you can commit to that schedule. Remember that you only want to post as often as you and your staff can reasonably commit to doing.

- *Is content really that important for my business if I'm a _____?*
    - Yes! It doesn't matter what industry you're in; if you're trying to grow your business, you need to be posting on a regular basis. There's no excuse not to; if you (yourself) don't have time, then it should be because you're busy with other customers and clients and, therefore, should be able to hire someone to do it for you.

Troubleshooting

- It's okay if you haven't been posting on a regular schedule, but you need to start as soon as possible. For example, Facebook keeps internal page scores for your business based on a percentage of engagement and consistency of your posts, so make sure you're on a schedule!
- If your content isn't quite perfect and needs a change of color, structure, or design help, that's okay too, but hire someone who's skilled in that area to help you because, again, the customer's perception is your reality.

Story

Imagine standing in a parking lot. On your right-hand side, you have a hole-in-the-wall restaurant with the best fried rice in the state; however, not many people know about it (including yourself in this scenario). On your left-hand side, you have PF Chang's that you've most likely heard of it if not been there. You can see that the PF Chang's building is brand-new, clean, and it looks like it might even have valet parking, *but* you know they charge almost four times as much for food that may not be half as good.

You may disagree now that the situation has been laid out, but most people will go to the PF Chang's simply because it looks better from the outside. The point of this story is that you can be the best _____ or sell the best _____ in the United States, but if the customers' perceptions are that of a hole-in-the-wall, they're going to choose your competitor by default, so make sure that your content not only draws people in but gives potential/existing customers a reason to tell their friends about you and your business.

Differentiate

Know the elements of your business that drive superior value and distinguish you against others market-actors. Then harness that driver in all you do. Differentiating yourself and your company from your competition always seems obvious to the business owner, but never to the audience or their employees.

For example, someone could Google Search "ice-cream shops near me" and have ten places come up. Let's say all of them have a four-star average review or higher, and let's say that the top three choices are all about a five-minute walk from the current location—how does your company win that race? Unique and clever business names can be catchy, but what does your online presence look like? If we assume someone has never seen, heard of, cared about, or even considered your business, your online presence will absolutely be their impression of you and your business. You can have the best ice cream in town, but if the photos of your business are pixelated, you have bad reviews, or your website could use a tune-up, why wouldn't this person choose the other two ice cream stores?

Again, we are in a buyer's market, so it's extremely important that business owners cater to every detail when differentiating themselves. If you can't find a way to differentiate from your competition, then you need to look within yourself and find how to brand you, the business owner, as a unique, compelling benefit to the buyer. This most always stems from personality traits and/or work experience.

Additionally, "Product" will be addressed later in this book; sometimes, the product or service is the differentiating factor, but this is extremely rare. In short, distance your company from your competitors, not your customers.

THE ADVERTISER'S ALPHABET

Here's what you need to do:

1. Market research and competitive intelligence; know what others in your industry are doing and know how they do it.
    a. Recognize marketing approaches from other businesses and try to assess if it's working.
    b. Know how savvy the customers are in your industry. For highly technical industries, the differentiators may be deep in the supply chain or operations of a company. Don't be afraid to lean in on these items if your client's customers share deep industry knowledge.
    c. Refresh often to stay relevant and protect against fluctuations.

2. List all the ways that your company is different from the large to the small. These are your differentiators:
    a. List the benefits and weakness of each.
        i. A few metrics to consider: ROI, customer capture, market share, and novelty.
        ii. Remember, just because it's different doesn't mean it's good (or bad). See ego.
    b. Look for synergies; do any of these differentiators tell a compelling story when together?
        i. For example, if you're a boutique liquor store with a storefront that looks like a gingerbread house, could you put together a story about being an adult candy store?

3. Tell the world. Once you know why your business is the best or the most meaningful to customers, don't make others look for it. Tell them. Tell them visually, verbally, in prose, and manner. Your differentiator should be a natural fit for your brand strategy.

Questions to Consider:

- *What are spending habits within your target market and community?*
    - Knowing your target market's spending habits (psychographic traits) will give you the competitive edge over the competition you're looking for; it's probable that you don't currently have this information.
        - There are databases filled with this type of information (try Google).
        - Google Analytics and Google Search Console are excellent tools for this.

- *What are people in your area been fond of recently? Are there any events going on within the community that you can sponsor or help out (publicly) in any way?*
    - Going back to the previous question, *gathering* (see Gather) psychographic information and *keeping* (see Keep) are foundational improvements you can make for the success of your business.
    - Sponsoring a local event (for charity) is a great way to *differentiate* yourself from the competition while also building rapport among your target market (as well as your cross-promotion partner's [sponsor's] audience).

Troubleshooting

- If you're having trouble finding ways to differentiate yourself from your competitors, that's normal at first. Instead of thinking about differentiation based on "we do this service" or "we don't do this service," think of it at a personal level.
    - What do your competitors' customer journeys look like — can you make them better?

- A good way of locating differentiators for your business is to write a list of everything you're currently doing that you know (for a fact) does *not* differentiate you.
  - Once you have this list, you and your team can look at it and add additional attributes and services.

Story

I have worked for many companies where this was overlooked and/or understated and seen the negative effects it can have on the business and its customers. With my business, I spent months figuring out a way to *cut through the noise* after being told by multiple people it couldn't be done in the advertising industry. I focused on what *every other company* was saying then said the exact opposite, and it easily won the attention of my target audience.

I wrote and rewrote my sales script until I had something called *The Golden Call*; now, the only objection I get from people I pitch it to is that they will get back to me when they can afford me; I spent time creating a *product* no one can say no to (see Product).

Ego

Your ego will kill any marketing strategy before it gets out of the gates if you're not careful. What you think is a good product or idea could be someone's worst nightmare, so use your ears and not your mouth when formulating a marketing strategy. Ego is not confidence; you should and must be confident in yourself and the work you produce. Ego is that nagging voice that tells you that you are right over and above all else; when you refuse to see other's views, recommendations, or experiences, like a horse with blinders on, ego can lead you to walk one path, missing the myriad avenues to differentiate message and brand. Ego is the *judgment* killer.

Data is king, so don't betray it. Let the numbers do the work. Remove your ego and let the data tell you what your customers and employees want to hear, see, touch, taste, and, yes, sometimes even smell. What primes them to click and then, even better, interact with your world? What makes them gravitate toward a product and choose it? It is about them, not you; remove hubris and be humble.

This section is a bit harsh because it needs to be, so we'll push through this section together. Identifying what not to do is easy, so what does a business owner do with their ego to serve their business? The first step is acknowledging all the people, employees, family, and friends that have helped you get where you are today. Acknowledgment comes in many forms, from formalized recognition software to taking the time to listen to your employee's drivers, offering a heartfelt thank you with inclusion of why you are grateful to work *with* them to putting their pay before your own.

Acknowledging these people and putting them, their lives, and their dreams in front of yours makes for some clean living. It isn't easy to do, but when you do it right on the hardest days, your employees will rally behind you and not only keep you in check but keep you, the leader, motivated. Put your energy into giving others positive energy, and the positivity will come back to you tenfold in due time if you keep your intentions pure.

So while your ego is most likely the reason that you have made it as far as you have, you must recognize and acknowledge those around you and lift them up. To outsiders, prospective employees, potential customers, and anyone learning about your business, what your employees are saying about you and your company will always outweigh what the business owner says as the truth, however, convoluted it may seem. Put your employees first, and your clients will put your company first.

Here's what you need to do:

1. If you are a business owner and do not have a therapist or some type of emotional outlet, I strongly advise seeking one out, whether it's by referral or a Google Search.
    a. Your personal problems will almost always reflect onto your personal work, so it is imperative that you preemptively prevent this from happening as often as possible.

2. Clearly define your personal goals away from your business's goals. Sometimes they overlap, but if you have employees involved, they should not be subject to your personal life and its goals/shortcomings.

3. After establishing a clear path and plan for your own personal development, help your employees do the same. As they say on the airplane, "in the event of an emergency, put your mask on before you help others."
    a. If you can't breathe, chances are you're taking up all the air in the room and leaving others around to suffocate.

Questions to Consider:

- *Why do my employees leave after I feel I've done everything for them?*
    - You can have an MBA from Harvard, but if you don't understand and connect with your employees, they're going to leave you; why wouldn't they?

- *Why do my clients leave after I've provided them with five-star service?*
    - Same story; if you don't take the time to connect and understand what your target audience's behaviors and interests are, you're shooting in the dark.

- *If I'm doing everything right, why do I have a hard time connecting with my staff and clients?*
    - It's extremely easy as a business owner to get caught up living in your own world. You are the master of your own universe, and that mindset has helped you achieve success, but if people are sticking with you, I highly recommend reexamining yourself and your human (resources) strategy for the betterment of your team and business.

Troubleshooting

- If you don't know where to start on this one, I highly recommend reading *The War of Art* by Steven Pressfield.
- Ego is one of the hardest things to manage when you have people that follow your orders on a daily basis; make sure you set aside time for appreciation of your team in the form of a fun event or some type of recognition period for your staff and clients.

Story

Egos are what usually and unfortunately get successful business owners to where they are, but they always hit a ceiling and can never seem to figure out why.

Time and time again, I have seen (what I call) *ego*-preneurs be their own biggest obstacle on their path to success. I'm going to err on the side of saying what to do rather than what not to do here, but please do not shut out new information, new people, new ideas, and new ways of thinking in the name of conserving your pride; it will likely be your downfall.

Use your *ego* to your benefit—but not in the way you might assume. Let your *ego* be a guiding light of two things: your stretch goals and how you want to be remembered.

Fluctuation

Market fluctuation is the only thing that can be guaranteed by any marketer, so prepare for it like your life and future of your business depends on it because it does. Don't get caught up playing a game of catch-up and making reactive edits to your business when you could have implemented positive proactive changes. Market fluctuations can skyrocket your business, and they can also end in a twenty-four-hour period if you don't have systems in place. Once you have systems in place (a five-star customer journey/experience), you can then adapt and change them to fit your current needs.

Fluctuations can occur because of change in season, change in client ownership, change in the direction of the wind, and whether or not it rained last Tuesday. In other words, there are some things that cannot be predicted, so all business owners can do is have systems in place that prevent the fluctuation from affecting the cash flow of your business. The term *market fluctuation* doesn't just refer to external changes in your sales, new leads, or revenue; it can also refer to social fluctuations. Things change, and so do people; what may have been acceptable behavior in the office last year could be completely socially taboo next year. What your employees considered to be a living wage two years ago could be putting them in poverty next year. What your employees considered a fair amount of paid leave per year may not be enough this year if they have taken on a larger workload and you have not given them a raise.

Long story short, if you are not keenly and currently aware of the fluctuations that can and/or will affect your business, you will become aware of them one way or another, so always *keep* (see Keep) tabs on socio-economic changes, especially in your business's service area.

THE ADVERTISER'S ALPHABET

Here's what you need to do:

1. Markets fluctuate, but your business doesn't have to; put in place a clearly defined sales process that you and your employees understand at 100 percent to eliminate the stress of the unknown.
    a. Once this is in place, your system illustrates whether or not your business is passing or failing for the week, month, or year.

2. Record and keep (see Keep) marketplace data, be it internal or external. If you know what was happening at this time of year (last year) with your business, you can somewhat safely assume an echo of the same will be happening this year.
    a. Instead of a reactionary process to problems and successes, maintain a proactive process to problems and successes, and the problems will seem much small, and the successes will seem much greater.

3. Announce on social media to your customers and followers that you are expecting a fluctuation in your sales or services in the coming month. Alternatively, create a seasonal or holiday-related offer to offset the expected fluctuations in your cash flow.
    a. Create reliability and sustainability in a world that is lacking, and people will want to work with you and work for you.

Questions to Consider:

- *What if I don't have any existing data on market fluctuation?*
    - A lot of businesses don't have existing data; it's never too late to start collecting data, so find a system that works and stick with it.

- *My business feels like an unpredictable rollercoaster when it comes to cash flow, and some months are completely dry; what can I do?*
    - Most business owners struggle with this. It's nothing to be ashamed of; having a system in place that documents incoming clients' and customers' information will help you sleep at night, so do it.

Troubleshooting

- Data collection is not fun; no one enjoys it. If you do it correctly, it's pen and paper mixed with hours spent on a spreadsheet, but someone has to do it, so get it done.

- Not having data comes with its own set of issues, but it's never too late to start. Put a system in place as soon as possible to record customers' ages, locations, genders, behaviors, interests, and lifetime customer value.
    - Lifetime customer value (LCV) is one of the four most important numbers in regard to growing your business and can be calculated several ways; "it's worth a Google."

Story

If I had a dollar for every time the market *fluctuated*, I wouldn't be writing this book. There will always be good months and bad months—days when you're better than you've ever been and days where you've achieved a new low, especially as a business owner. The highs and lows don't matter; what matters is that you (the business owner) are consistent throughout each day, week, and month that you're leading your team to inevitable victory. The same concept applies to your clients/customers and their successes and failures; their lives and their businesses will *fluctuate*, so it is up to you to provide consistency and clarity.

Gather

Gather as much data as humanly possible before starting any advertising campaign unless you're okay with throwing money out the window on data collection using paid advertising campaigns. *Know the ages, genders, locations, incomes, behavior, and interests of your existing customers so that you can create a target audience profile based on that information.*

Use these profiles to target, retain, and upsell customers. Gathering data sets from multiple, unique entities allows you to compare those data sets. Utilize internal and external data sources for identity, sales, engagement, attitudinal, and behavioral datasets. Revisit that market research and competitive intelligence you gathered when setting up the strategy that you refresh often. And depending on your purpose, it may be worth accessing paid consumer databases and business databases.

When you have matching data sets from multiple sources, it is safer to say that the information is accurate. This collection and assessment are doing your due diligence. When you have peace of mind that your data sets are accurate, the marketing strategy creates itself. Every move you make should be based on the data. What data depends on your business. For some business owners, the most important growth factor is revenue, and for some, the most important growth factor is awareness, so data will dictate how either of these situations play out. For example, if your client wants to be seen as a trusted advisor, awareness campaigns built on page view drivers and emails with the highest click-through rates will be more fruitful than building campaigns to maximize conversion rates.

Once you gather data, you can gather people, and once you gather people, you have an audience. If you've done your due diligence, this audience should be full of people that are extremely interested in your products and/or services (see Product); you've positioned yourself as a reliable source for news and information in your industry, so keep gathering so you can keep sharing!

Here's what you need to do:

1. Quite literally, gather as much existing and previous client data as you can, whether it's invoices, receipts, patient files, notebooks—it doesn't matter. You want to come out of this process with an average age, gender, income, amount spent with you, and location of people that you are working with or have worked with; this is considered demographic information. Additionally, you'll want to get as much psychographic data as you can (this information is much more difficult to obtain but is worth its weight in marketing gold). This type of data includes things like behaviors and interests of your clients and customers.
    a. Once you have gathered and organized this data, you can then plug it into any marketing campaign and save yourself what would potentially be thousands of dollars on market testing (to find your target audience).

2. Gather your employees for a morning meeting every weekday or, at the very least, once per week. Gathering for a meeting allows you (the business owner) to clearly define the goals for that day, week, or month (you should also have a monthly meeting the first week of each month to lay out goals for that month).
    a. When everyone is on the same page, everyone wins—not just you and your team but the clients as well. Communication is the single, most important key to success, whether it's your front desk administrator communicating with clients or it's you, the business owner communicating with your team; everyone needs to be on the same page and under

the same understanding of the tasks and goals at hand.

3. Gather your clients and customers for an appreciation dinner or party; you don't have to spend a fortune on food and drinks; the fact that you're doing it shows you care.
    a. This is especially important for doctor's offices and other types of businesses where you are addressing someone's personal life as a service. You'd be surprised at what some people consider to be "addressing their personal life." For instance, a hairdresser or barber can almost act as a therapist for some people. Another unorthodox example would be a fashion designer or interior designer; if you're affecting someone's home, life, car, or anything family-related, you have the ability to go the extra mile and provide some type of reciprocation for their work with you, so do it.

Questions to Consider:

- *Is there such a thing as too much data, too many meetings, or too much preparation?*
    - Actually, yes, there absolutely is such a thing. It's great to start gathering data, gathering for meetings on a regular basis, and creating a synergistic workplace using these strategies, but don't lose sight of the bigger picture. For example, if your mandatory morning meeting is getting in the way of client work, cancel the meeting for that day.
        - The same goes with data; it's great to collect data, but if the metaphor for your data collection is that of "a pile of legal boxes in the hall closet," you should consider reexamining your tracking measures and data collection strategy so that it is conducive

to your desired outcome or your "bigger picture" goal.

- *What if my employees all work remotely?*
    - Unless you operate a brick-and-mortar business that requires in-person work, I highly recommend being some type of advocate for the work-from-home model.
        - Finding the way to motivate your employees can be an arduous task depending on what industry you're in, how long they've been working with you, and what their normal interests and behaviors are; it's important to ask about these things when hiring so that you know and can rely on them.

- Another good way to find out how to motivate them is by simply asking them what would make working for you a better experience; some people won't say anything; reward the ones who do so that others will start doing it. You'll then create an environment where employees feel they can share what they want without fear of losing their jobs.

Troubleshooting

- There's a lot that can go wrong (very quickly) when it comes to trying to gather your team and find out what they want at the same time. So plan it out as best as possible with your leadership team or if you are the leadership team, consult with outside colleagues in a related industry.
- When gathering and collecting data on your business, make sure to do it right the first time; I've worked with clients where we've had to backtrack, and it's a time suck as well as a potential drain on finances via opportunity cost.

Story

There once was a time in which I did *not* spend time *gathering* my information and research before starting on a project; let's just say those days are over. While working with a Fortune 50 company on an ad campaign, my entire job was research, preparation, and presentation of findings so that when the campaign was implemented, it would be directed to the right audience at the right time. We constructed multiple surveys, ran focus groups, and compiled secondary research (research from other sources) into a presentation that ended up changing their entire messaging strategy for the given campaign. In other words, reliable data changes the game.

Habit

Following routine, normalized regular cadence, and practice of work transforms potential energy into action. Rather than having information siloed in one executive's head or in that one random notebook, having good habits in place allows all employees access to up-to-date, usable, and accessible information. Consistency is key, and the money is in the habits you create for yourself and your business.

The strategies that bring in the most ROI for small business owners are some of the simplest in existence; it's simply a question of who is going to do the work. Yes, you can hire someone to do it for you, but let's use writing content as an example. Let's say you hire a writer that charges $500 per hour (someone that knows what they're doing), and you have them write content for you. Sounds like a good idea, right? Well, in every case I've seen, this is actually a break point.

At the end of the day, the business owner or a longtime employee is the only people that really know the nitty-gritty details of your business; they're the only people that know the real story of the business. So someone inside the business needs to make a habit of writing content. Once the content is written, it can always be polished by an expert, but the story needs to come from the people who know the business. Forming habits around content creation is key to the success of any marketing campaign.

As with anything, the power of habit is a key factor in how successful the business owner will become with their marketing strategy. Too many times, I've heard of business owners being promised what are essentially delusions of grandeur. You are likely creating a marketing strategy to increase revenue, grow market share, or increase brand awareness. You might find this work boring, tedious, and time-consuming. But if you are tempted to assign out these tasks, be careful. There is no magic marketing plan that will save your business. You have to put in the work, and that work is more effective and efficient if it's built on top of good habits.

Here's what you need to do:

1. Create workflow habits for your team and make sure that they are easy to understand.

2. Create revenue analysis habits; if you don't know your monthly revenue off the top of your head, you need to; you can't fix what you can't see.

3. Suggest habits for your clients and customers and give them an easy-to-understand routine that allows them to work with you on a regular basis without interrupting their daily lives.
    a. Create a system that allows them to be themselves and live their lives but accentuates your gratitude for them working with you.

Questions to Consider:

- *Can I create habits on behalf of someone?*
    - No—be careful with this one. Be careful not to force preconceived notions onto people because they are hard to be undone; you can suggest them, but don't force them. It's nonsensical.

Troubleshooting

- Decide your best time of day and build your habits around that most productive. Writing activities or those you build into habits do not need to utilize your prime thinking hours. Leave that productive time to creative and analytical work.

Story

    Habits are like hair; everyone has them, but some people have bad hair—I mean, *habits*. My schedule is that of a digital clock; I never miss a beat, and it's important that I don't to ensure my clients' successes. The best advice I can give here is that if you don't make your bed when you wake up in the morning, you're doing it wrong. Making your bed is the most important task of the day. I don't care if you sleep on the couch; when you wake up, make sure your bed is in pristine condition because it's the first task of the day. Once you complete the first task of the day (and it's pristine), you can move on to your other tasks and make sure those tasks are also pristinely completed. Boom—you're now having a great day!

Illuminate

Illuminating other people is one of the best ways to get your word out. *By publicly illuminating others on your business's social media accounts during in-person meetings and other communication-centered events, you position yourself as an expert by creating a comparison scenario and highlighting what the other entity is amazing at doing.* Host a podcast and invite a client for a discussion about their business. During that conversation, you're highlighting their industry expertise, and you are gaining benefits of association with that industry. The next time someone thinks of a marking specialist in relation to said industry, they're primed to think of your company. To make the conversation evermore beneficial, cross-promote the podcast with influencers and others in the industry who share your target audience, client bases, and followings. Give them content, and they will lead business to you.

A graphic designer should highlight their clients' success stories by displaying their work for others to see. Not only should they share the work they did but they should tell the story of the work. If you *illuminate* others within your business or life story, people will be able to relate to you and will seek you out as the product or service they want in their lives. The person you *illuminate* should always be different from the last person so that you can *illuminate* as many different cultures, backgrounds, and personalities to formulate a holistic story of your brand and messaging strategy. Be selfless in everything that you and your business do, and the results will come in due time. Nothing happens overnight with marketing strategies, nor should it, so spend time with other people in similar industries and get the word out organically. In turn, you will then be able to continue *illuminating* new partners and people as they begin working with you. This work will become a business *habit* (see Habit) and pay dividends while building your network and reputation.

THE ADVERTISER'S ALPHABET

Here's what you need to do:

1. Create and define a system that your employees can easily understand that allows your business to illuminate and spotlight clients and customers on a routine basis.
    a. Whether it's social media, a podcast, a philanthropic event, or a birthday party, don't be afraid to put your client or customer of the month in the spotlight; people will always respond more positively to a business or entity highlighting someone else than if it were simply talking about themselves or itself.

2. Illuminate your employees; this doesn't have to be on social media, but it should be (at the very least) known amongst your other employees. If an employee hears that they're doing well, but no one else on the team hears it, it is possible (if not probable) that the employee in question will assume it wasn't said at all.

3. Illuminate new products and services in advance of their actual launch date so that clients, customers, and employees all have time to plan for its arrival. It's great to have surprises at birthday parties, but if no one hears about a new product or service before it's actually released, then they have plenty of time to start working with or buy from someone else—a.k.a., your competition.

Questions to Consider:

- *In what format should I Illuminate someone?*
    - Using social media as a catalyst for *illumination* is a great idea, but don't forget to actually do the *illuminating*; posting a photo of someone and waving goodbye moments later does not count as public relations.

- *Are there certain times in which illumination is not the solution?*
    - Yes—do not be careless with your power to illuminate someone; it can be taken away far faster than the years you've spent *gathering* (see Gather) and garnering your reputation; be genuine.
        - *Genuine was a word that was strongly considered as replacing the word gather for the letter G, but we have truth for that.*

Troubleshooting

- You should *always* ask someone before doing something like this; never assume someone wants to be *illuminated*; you can get in trouble quickly.
- Always plan out your *illuminations* (preferably for the foreseeable [next] ninety days). If you have them written and planned, you can easily deviate from them if needed; when you don't have them planned—let's not go there.

Story

After working with hundreds of business owners, I can tell you from experience that the people that illuminate others in their work do much better than those who repeatedly showcase themselves. For instance, Staci Danford, MBE, founder of The Grateful Brain, a business based on gratitude's positive effect on the human brain, does an excellent job of this; you should ask her for advice if you're having trouble in this realm.

Judgment

Understand and accept the judgment. Judgment comes from every direction: internal, external, and the self. Everyone wants to tell you how your actions should change, how your words could be different, and how your thinking needs to adapt. It's easy to have an opinion after the fact when it's not your work being judged.

The Bad News

Every marketing strategy involves putting out messaging to the masses, whether directly through chosen campaigns or indirectly through the daily actions of staff, clients, and yourself. Understanding and accepting that judgment comes along with the job. There is no way to make everyone happy, but there is a way to make yourself happy and keep yourself happy. People are people, and they will always have opinions. But they do not have the perspective you have or know the plan you've set into motion. This view is important to understand whether you're a solopreneur, a Fortune 500 CEO, or a high school student looking to expand their skill set.

If you want to make strides as a business owner, you have to be able to make decisions plain and simple. Decision-making power comes from brainpower, and you only have so much brain power, so don't waste any on sorting out whether or not person x, y, or z judged you at the last company dinner, for the most recent social media post, or what someone said on your last call. There's no way around it; people are going to judge you. The key is staying focused on your work. Decision fatigue is real, and it will come no matter what; make a choice here to not let others' judgment push you to that point prematurely.

ANDREW HINDLE

The Good News

I never mentioned all the judgments that come from all the amazing people you have in your circle, your client base, and your target audience (if you're doing it right). If you truly believe in what you sell, you should be able to easily take a look at your products and yourself without caring about the judgments of other people. Remember those positive perspectives from others, the data you've gathered, and the market research you've done. If you don't believe in what you sell, that's okay, but find a way to make it better, make people like it, and make it worthwhile. If you read reviews, approach comments with a neutral attitude (remember ego) and think if taking those recommendations would improve your product or services.

Sometimes small changes can make big improvements without big investments. Look at it as an opportunity to accommodate and respond to customers. If you need to repackage something, repackage it. Alter language, adapt imagery, or physically repackage a product if it's easy and feedback dictates it's truly a problem. Repackage it not only for your clients but for yourself so that you can achieve clarity of purpose.

Here's what you need to do:

1. Take a step back and ask yourself what *judgments* you have made recently and write them down. Are you aware that you made them, or did they happen subconsciously?
    a. Are these *judgments* that you are proud of affected your business, employees, or clients in a negative or positive way?

2. Write a list of positive *judgments* you can make in the next thirty days and to whom they will be given.
    a. Also, consider whether or not they need to be publicized or if they can be *judgments* kept to yourself.

The Only Question to Consider:

- *Are my or my team's judgments helping or hurting my business?*
  - If they're hurting your business, I highly recommend hiring someone to coach you through the difficulties; the longer you wait, the worse the outcome(s) will be.

Troubleshooting

- If you don't know if your *judgments* are helping or hurting you, chances are that they are hurting your business, and you should seek help from a business coach or therapist. If you have unaddressed personal problems, they are almost always sure to reflect on your business.

Story

I have seen *judgment* from and about all ages and walks of life; it never adds value to the bigger picture or the stretch goal. Everyone judges consciously and subconsciously, but there's a difference between thinking it and saying it. Instead of thinking about *judgment* with a negative connotation, think of it as a positive way to build and inspire the people around you. Be the change you want to see and vocalize your positive *judgments* about the work and people around you. You will start to see positive reactions from team members and those around you; in time, those around you will also start to positively *judge* the work and people around them. People tend to act like how they're treated, so judge them with good intentions, and they are more likely to respond with good work and behavior.

Keep

Everything you do needs to be organized and backed up at least twice for your business. Even if it seems inconsequential, keep records of every client interaction, every sale, and every strategy change. Miscommunications will get you killed before you get out of the gate, and miscommunications most always stem from a lack of organization, which stems from a lack of keeping records on every move you make with every client. Use some form of customer-relationship-management (CRM) software because this ties directly to your customer experience. Additionally, when you keep records of your clients' demographic and, if possible, psychographic information (use Google Analytics), you can create a spreadsheet that contains a list of your customers' age, gender, location, and affinity categories (what do they like to do/identify with) that will serve as your average customer's target audience profile.

Keep tabs on your employees' and clients' well-being. This is one of the most overlooked actions that I have seen throughout my professional career. Keep tabs on your employees by understanding what makes them tick, what they like to do, and what their strengths and weaknesses are. Keep track of your clients' well-being by asking them how they're doing. Keeping notes on their interests, family members, and other quirky information. Notes will help you remember what they have told you and will help you spark interesting conversations. By remembering details, your clients will know that you care.

Here's what you need to do:

1. Create a system that allows you to easily *keep* records on customer, employee, and business data.
    a. Even if it's an Excel Spreadsheet, this is better than nothing.

2. Keep up to date with changes in your employees' and clients' lives.
    a. This is important if you want to keep client and employee retention as high as possible.
    b. Get to know your constituents; they'll notice and appreciate you for it.

Questions to Consider:

- *What if I don't know where to start because my records are in disarray?*
    - This is perfectly normal; it's never too late to start keeping records the correct way. Salvage what you can and start keeping track of things in your new system.

- *What if my employees or clients don't want me involved in their personal lives?*
    - You don't have to be involved in their personal lives to *keep* track of them; you only have to show that you care about them. They'll tell you what they want to tell you, just don't forget what they tell you because they will remember everything you say.

Troubleshooting

- If your records are a mess, and you don't have records on your employees in any way whatsoever, this isn't uncommon, but it's imperative that you start doing it, so take it seriously; your employees will, whether you do or not.

Story

As many people have before me, I learned this the hard way. It should go without saying that keeping records, backups, and customer data is an obvious task, but time and time again, I see it gets overlooked, and it always comes back to bite. I have found tons of success using Dropbox Business and Google Drive as the storage unit for all my files. I could set my laptop and desktop on fire right now, and all my files would be safe; all I have to do is go buy a new computer and install Dropbox, and login to Google Drive. Start thinking of your laptop or computer as a proxy instead of a file cabinet. Store everything in the cloud so you can stop worrying about files on your computer. This is also important for scaling because it's easy to create share-access to files for new employees.

Luck

Recognize your luck and know when to use it. Believe it or not, everyone is lucky in one way or another; it's about having the eye for opportunities and what you do with those opportunities that matter. Another interpretation of luck could be viewed statistically, but I like to look at it from the opportunity angle. When something bad happens, doors close, people leave, and someone gets upset. But what happens after those doors close? As long as you keep moving, you'll probably run into another doorway, but when viewed as an opportunity to help others, grow your business and become a leader of your industry; you should consider yourself extremely lucky to be alive and have the chances that you were given, however minor or major those may be.

Here's what you need to do:

1. Start looking for positive things to say about yourself, your employees, and your clients, and doors will open for you.

2. Create your own luck by manifesting your business's success using the opportunities you currently have in front of you.
    a. Make the most of what you currently have, and better opportunities will present themselves by default.

3. If something you perceive as "negative" happens, always try to look for the silver lining and turn this "negative" into a possible opportunity!

Questions to Consider:

- What are you talking about? You sound insane.
  - My belief system is *karma* for a few reasons that I won't get into, but I can promise you that you get out of the universe what you put into it, whether it's bad or good—it's simply a matter of time, so start putting in good and start getting good out.

Troubleshooting

- There isn't much I can do to help with this one. It's a choice that has to be made within yourself, and this book nor any other book is going to make that choice for you.
  - If you're still at a loss, try a therapist or some meditation.

Story

    I used to think I was the unluckiest person on earth. I can tell you from experience that the world is *not* out to get you, nor anyone for that matter; it doesn't have time. These days, I create my own luck. You can call it *luck,* but I prefer to think of it as opportunism. All we have are opportunities; it's what we do with them that makes us *lucky* or *unlucky.* So next time you are presented with a choice outside of your normal routine, treat it like a golden opportunity for positive change in your life.

Messaging

You can be as slick as you want, but there will always be people that see your true motives, so keep them clean if you want longevity and profitability from your business. *Make your motive public information so that people can relate to you and your business at a foundational level.* Make sure that everyone working for you not only understands your messaging strategy but is in agreement with it. All it takes is one person to sway an audience, so make sure the people on the inside are visibly and verbally on board with the strategy; this mainly includes your employees.

Once you have your team on board with your messaging strategy, your marketing campaign is one step closer to running itself. It's safe to assume that everything your team says and does is being recorded; this is why having a stated and outlined *messaging* strategy is so important; it does the preventative maintenance for you. When everyone is on board with the *messaging*, you can be confident that it will represent your *brand* with authenticity and reliability, which will keep your *brand* moving forward without the need for micromanagement; everyone wins.

Here's what you need to do:

1. Decide on a messaging strategy for your business or corporation.
2. Add listings to as many listing websites as possible.
3. Develop the message through spherical branding. Make sure you have consistency across all four factors below,

and these are woven across all areas; you prompt your message.
- a. Brand Vision
    - i. Have clarity of the brand vision or mantra. It should answer the "what" and "why" of your brand.
- b. Brand Position
    - i. Make sure your reputation is positioning your brand effectively.
- c. Brand Personality
    - i. Establish your brand's personality. What are the three-six characteristics that define your brand? These should be characteristics that match the way you share your message as well as the message itself. For example, if you position your brand as leading-edge, make sure you are using modern outreach approaches.
- d. Brand Club
    - i. Develop a cult-like following and a need for your product. Get reviews working for you. Give discounts or rewards to start capturing the word-of-mouth factor.

4. Ensure your story is authentic, different, and consistent (see Story).

Questions to Consider:

- *What should my messaging strategy be based on?*
    - Ideally, you would have records on previous PR campaigns and experiences, and you can base your new messaging strategy on this data, but if

not, then you will need to start *keeping* (See Keep) records on this so that you can make data-driven decisions for your business.
- It should also be based on your target audience's behaviors and interests; you don't want to have a messaging strategy geared toward twenty-five-year-olds if you are advertising for a retirement home; use your best *judgment* (see Judgment).

- *How do I know what to say and when to say it?*
  - No one knows what to say or when to say it (although there are plenty of people who claim they do); this is why having data is so important.
  - Get an understanding of your target audience, and it will become clear what you need to be saying to them.

- *What if my messaging strategy pisses people off, and I lose followers or constituents?*
  - You may have already noticed, but there's no way to please everyone; you're going to lose followers with any new *messaging* strategy; it's the cost of doing business in today's world.
  - For instance, if you're running an email campaign, and you see that you have a 22 percent open rate on your emails, an 8 percent unsubscribe rate, and 70 percent unopened, consider only targeting that 22 percent who opened on your next campaign.
    - Also, keep in mind that it is extremely common and often overlooked that the people who are liking, sharing, and following your content are not always the people who are paying you for your services, so make sure you have a clearly defined desired outcome for your campaign's *messaging* strategy.

Troubleshooting

1. Define your target audience using existing data.
2. Utilize the free space. Use free media spaces to operate at the highest level of cost and time efficiency.
    a. Listings: Google My Business, Yelp, Bing Places, and Apple Maps.
    b. Social Media: Facebook, Instagram, and LinkedIn.
    c. Habit: Schedule one hour every Thursday or Friday to post updates to these accounts and listings to optimize results.
3. Make sure Google Data Studio is set up for your website (data collection).
4. Create content based on the data.

Story

Messaging strategies are like butts; some people know exactly where theirs is, and others have no idea. I have spent years crafting my *messaging* strategy for my business, and it's constantly changing, and that's okay. When I think about my *messaging* strategy, I think about my target audience, my goals, and why I want to reach my target audience. Is what I want to say applicable, helpful, and relevant to my audience? Does it move me closer to my goal? Messaging strategies aren't just for marketing campaigns; when you meet someone (off the clock), you are still talking to them and, therefore, sending out a *message*. If the *message* is misinterpreted or disliked by the receiver of the message, the fault lies in the sender of the *message*, so be careful with what you say, be it positive or negative.

No

Protect the longevity of your brand and of your business through the power of "No." Saying *no* to things is a way of saying *yes* to yourself and your goals. So why don't you do it more? Saying *no* not only gives you freedom but it positions you as someone who is in control of their own future. You choose where you spend your energy, and *you* (see You) can focus on the actions that are the most rewarding. Free up time on your schedule by saying *no* to things that don't serve your goals and be choosy with your time. As you practice saying *no*, your business's growth strategy (as well as other aspects of life) becomes clarified and simplified. Focus on yourself and your business; you did the work to become a pro in your industry, so act like one; your time is valuable!

Saying *no* to employees can be one of the hardest things you will ever do as a leader, but it can also be one of the most important things you do for the success of your business. Employees that have devoted their time to your company deserve their piece of the pie (equity), and they deserve to be treated with the highest level of respect, just don't let them run you ragged or abuse their privileges; you will look like a weak leader, and that will attract more people looking to take what you've earned.

Alternatively, you can also look at this situation from a "what do I say 'yes' to" rather than a "when do I start saying 'no' to" situation. Again, making a list of your goals is extremely important (even if they're short-term). In either case, make sure that you are crystal clear on what you decide to do so that each time you say *yes* or *no*, you are moving closer to your desired outcome. Keep your goals front of mind to stay on the right path for your business.

Saying no to things doesn't always look like (literally) saying the word no. Sometimes, it means not responding to the salesman who has followed up for the tenth time; sometimes, it looks like taking a day off work, and other times, it looks like saying yes to fun things that you would've normally say no to.

Here's what you need to do:

1. Make a list of things that you are currently doing on a daily basis—everything in your business life and personal life.
    a. Once you have the list and you can see what your life looks like (on paper), it's much easier to look at things in a logical light; feel free to start crossing things off; if you have found your way into something (you want out of), you can find your way out.

Questions to Consider:

- *What if I've already said yes to something, and I can't get out of it easily?*
    - No problem—we've all been there. Create an exit strategy and start working your way there. There's no time like the present to audit your current commitments and make changes to benefit your business.

- *What if people don't like me or my business because I start saying no to them when I would've normally said yes?*
    - As written in *messaging* (email campaigns), there is a cost of doing business that relates to protecting you and your employees' mental health, and it's imperative that you protect it; no one will do it for you.

Troubleshooting

- If you're having trouble figuring out where to start with this because you've already committed to so many things that you feel like a prisoner in your own life, you're not alone. The key is to make these changes one *yes* or one *no* at a time.

Story

When you learn how to say *no* properly, your life will become a simplified version of itself, and your goals will be clearer as well as more obtainable. When you say *yes* to everyone all the time, you create a whirlwind of tasks that I've never seen anyone be able to keep up with; you don't want to do that to yourself, especially when trying to start a business. So start with something small; it gets easier. When you back it with sound reasoning, the people that keep asking you for things outside the spectrum of your work will stop and begin to respect your time.

Oath

When you decide to grow your business, you're making an oath to yourself to become the best version of yourself. You're making an oath to your employees to help them become the best versions of themselves. Additionally, I strongly recommend making an *oath* to whatever your higher power or belief system is; you don't have to be religious, but it is vital that you believe in something bigger than yourself (from my experience). Keep in mind that making an *oath* and *keeping* an *oath* are two (very) different things; don't be afraid to do the boring work; the money is in the consistency. When you take the *oath* to grow your business, you obtain clarity of purpose. The reasons you're in the game become obvious, and that makes all the difference when you start getting objections (see Judgment) and have to navigate the waters of sales.

Making an *oath* to yourself helps you find a line between saving the world and making money. It's easy to portray the mindset of "I'm doing this to help people," and the reality of the situation may be that you need to help yourself first. You can make an *oath* within your business to only work with women, only work with special needs, or only work with whatever group of people you want to help. Nonprofits are experts at drawing the line between what you can say and what you can deliver; they have to be. It's important to understand the difference between what you want to promise people versus what you can actually do. It's okay to have a gap between the two but make sure you're able to close that gap or are actively learning how to close the gap. If you're having trouble closing the gap, try thinking of promises or commitments you have made that are currently withstanding, and find out how you can finish what was started. When you follow through on your commitments, you start to consistently provide a five-star customer experience and fulfill your *oath* to your employees and target audience, which increases revenue and decreases turnover.

Here's what you need to do:

1. Make a list of your current promises to yourself, however concrete or abstract they may be.
    a. Some may be as simple as "get my oil changed by the end of the month," and some might be as complex as "increase my revenue three times by the end of the quarter."

2. Have your employees write down their *oaths* to themselves (in respect to their careers).
    a. Once they've made their lists, you can hold a semi-fun meeting and discuss them and help each other move closer to your goals; you never know who might be holding the key to your success (in most cases, it's *you* [see You]).

Questions to Consider:

- *Do I need to make my oath(s) known to my clients and employees?*
    - No, but you should. As if you were going into battle, your troops need something to rally behind, and the best leaders are in front of their army, not behind it, so I recommend making it known.

- *Can I make an oath on behalf of my employees?*
    - You can, but if you haven't vetted them to see if their values (see Value) align with yours, then you could be making a grave mistake that could cause disarray within your company down the road.

- Make sure you *gather* (see Gather) your employees to discuss this before committing to any strategy.

Troubleshooting

- Making *oaths* to yourself, your employees, and your business is tough because it's almost impossible to uphold all your promises as a business owner. This is why it's so important to be picky and selective with the *oaths* you choose to make, regardless of whether it's to you or your staff; plan for the worst and hope for the best.

Story

I have made promises and *oaths* to myself multiple times and failed myself because of it. It is extremely important to be specific and realistic with what *oaths* that you make to yourself, your employees, and your business. Oaths should only be made once research and data analysis have been finished. You should also have a metric for your *oaths* to measure your success; if you can't measure and track your progression or regression, you'll never know if you're actually moving forward. Treat oaths as if they are written in stone once they are made; especially as a business owner, you are only as good as your word, whether it's to your employees, your customers, or yourself (see You), so be deliberate with your *oaths*.

Product

Developing and defining the right product for your business takes time, so get comfortable. Having a product that no one (in your target audience) can say *no* to makes life much easier when you start trying to make sales; trust me on this one. Many times, I have heard people say, "There is no way to cut through the noise," meaning there is no way to stand out amongst your competition; this isn't true. If you can't or don't stand out from your competition, you either haven't created the right product, or you haven't yet found how to correctly position and brand your existing product properly within the marketplace.

The solution has always, is always, and will always be in existence; all you have to do is find it. Once you find and package your product or service properly, the clients come to you, your word-of-mouth referral basis grows, and you become the leader of your industry and a recognized authority among your target market. In some cases, the business owner *is* the product, which means that you (the business owner) need to spend time perfecting yourself and your brand. *This is the case with many service-industry business owners who also act as public speakers.*

When you are the product, your communication and messaging strategies will almost certainly determine the level of success you will see as a solopreneur. Illustrating a clear plan on what you should and will be saying to your audience will help guide you through the tricky ocean of sales. Customers need to get a consistent five-star customer experience every time they interact with you or your brand so that they can create a positive association with your brand (and want to tell their friends). Once you create positive associations with your product and brand, the company will start to take care of itself. Just make sure that you are individualizing your client experiences; people want to be seen as individuals, not client number four thousand.

When you are not the product, guess what? Your communication and messaging strategies become even more important and complex because you are now guiding a multitude of individuals on what to say, when to say, and how to say it; this is much more difficult; however, the solution remains the same. Write out a clear plan and stick to it.

Here's what you need to do:

1. Create a list of all your products and services—including pricing and average timeframe someone works with you for that specific product or service.
    a. Once you have this list, you'll be able to add it to the collection of the other lists I've hounded you about making earlier in this book, and you'll start to *gather* and *keep* solid set of records for your business!

2. Highlight the products or services that are currently bringing in the most money on a reliable basis, and use a different color for the products or services that may not currently be bringing in money, but you want them to at some point; this will start to give you a game plan for your success!

Questions to Consider:

- *What if I don't have a product, and I'm in the service industry?*
    - Your service is your product, so perfect your service!

- *What if I don't know how to perfect my product?*
    - I'd try googling "Stacked Deck Advertising;" I hear they do decent work.

- *What if I spend time perfecting my product and it doesn't sell?*
    - This happens, but don't let it stop you or slow you down. If a product fails, it just means you need to make a new one or a better one that's more aligned with your target market; don't give up!

Troubleshooting

- Just like Thomas Edison and the light bulb, it's going to take you more than one try to make a perfect *product*, so don't get discouraged by failures.
    - As long as you're *keeping* data, your failures will actually be the road to your success.

- I've seen people get mixed up between creating a perfect product and marketing a product. These are two different things that should not be done at the same time.
    - For instance, it's difficult and more expensive to market a product that hasn't been perfect, whereas, if you have perfect your *product*, it should sell itself, and then it's simply a matter of spreading the word!

Story

I spent years mastering and perfecting my *product*. I work in an extremely saturated market; almost every business owner works in a saturated market these days. I was once told that "there is no way to cut through the noise, it's just a numbers game, so pick up the phone and make more calls" (in reference to getting more clients). To me, that seemed like a problem that hadn't been solved, a cop-out. While it is important to work hard, it is also imperative that you work smart if you want to make strides in your competitive market. After about eighteen months of deliberation, I finally found a way to cut through the noise; it came to me in the form of a sales script for phone calls to potential clients. Since then, my mission has been clear, and I can talk to anyone about my services, the cost, and the results that can be expected. Once you perfect your *product*, you shouldn't have to pick up the phone; people will come to you.

Quotable

If everything in your marketing campaign isn't top to bottom *quotable*, then you need to rethink your strategy. *Word travels quite quickly these days, so make sure that everything you, your employees, and, by default, your company puts out is press friendly.* Public relations (a.k.a. your *messaging* strategy) are important; once your reputation is tainted, it's nearly impossible to recover.

Not only does your marketing strategy's *messaging* need to be *quotable* but so do *you* (see You). Assume that everything you say and do will be heard, recorded, written down, and shared, so make sure that any time you are interacting with clients or employees, it's safe to assume that you are interacting with the world, including the people who are already your customers and the people who aren't. You will run into people that go out of their way to negate what you're saying; don't let this affect what you're doing. As long as you remain steadfast in your *messaging* and communications, people will follow you or get out of your way.

Being *quotable* not only ensures you have a solid reputation but it assures your target audience that you are a reliable, trustworthy source for information about your product or service. Being *quotable* is a good thing and (with how quickly word travels these days) should be practiced whether you're a business owner or not. Potential clients and customers will come to you for advice regarding your product or service and share the knowledge you give them with their friends, family, and colleagues, so make sure what they're sharing is worth repeating if you care about your reputation and business.

Here's what you need to do:

1. Audit your social media accounts for things that aren't *quotable*.
    a. If you see something that doesn't align with your current *messaging* strategy, just delete it. When building a business and a *brand*, everything you do, say, and probably even think will be viewed by someone at one time or another; it's inevitable.

2. Practice being *quotable* in your daily life.
    a. Whether it's with your spouse or a room full of people you don't know, always try to be the best version of yourself, and others will see you as a leader, thus, increasing your following and, by default, your revenue.

Questions to Consider:

- *What if I have said things in the past that aren't quotable?*
    - We all have done this; sometimes, it's best to completely rebrand and rename a business if you have gone too far down a dark road.

- *How will I know if something I or my business is saying is quotable?*
    - Say it out loud; does it sound like something you would like or want to hear?

Troubleshooting

- If you're having trouble figuring out if what you're saying is *quotable*, try asking a friend or colleague if what you're saying is good for the health of your business. Never assume anything.

- If you simply don't have anything to say at all and you're trying to figure out where to start, try coming up with a few adjectives to describe what you want people to see your business as.
  - From there, try fitting those adjectives into sentences describing your business. Pretty soon, you'll be conversational and *quotable* at the same time!

Story

I wish everything I said wasn't recorded, displayed on the internet, and/or shared with the world, but it is. Now, more than ever, it is important to be cognizant of every word you say, whether it's written, spoken, or even a thought. Start living as though you are always in front of and speaking to your target audience. Live a *quotable* life, and people will want to *quote* you more often. Don't act genuine and nice; *be* genuine and nice. If it's something you struggle with, that's okay; start small, and it will get easier with time.

Referrals

Referrals are the type of clients that every business owner wants. Referrals are way more likely to convert into a paying customer than someone from the internet who has never heard about your product or services, and they are much easier to deal with in terms of client interaction than someone who has been persuaded by an ad to use your product or service.

So how do you get more referrals for your business? It all starts with amazing content. Content can come in many different forms, but it should always have an educational or philanthropic aspect to it; people don't want to be sold to, so instead, teach them about what you do in brief segments. When you do this, you will be more likely to be top-of-mind (the first person they think of) when they have a problem that you can solve. When someone sees your content, hears about your content, or interacts with your content, the business owner or your staff (in-person content), that person becomes educated and qualified to speak about your business. When they're educated about your business, they're way more likely to tell other people about your products and services, which is the foundational goal for every advertising strategy.

Maximize your referrals' efficiency by creating a list of referral partners. Having a trusted network of referral partners allows you to focus on your business while your referral partners keep your pipeline of potential new clients full. However, you do not want to solely rely on any one source of new clients. Successful businesses (of all sizes) should have at least three inbound strategies. For instance, you could be knocking on doors, be running Google Ads, and have referral partners.

Once you have at least three to five trustworthy and reliable referral partners, you can start running cross promotions between businesses, creating a synergistic effect across the board everyone involved. If you are a mechanic, this would mean that you put flyers up in your shop for one of your referral partners showcasing their services and even offering a discount for mentioning the flyer. This gets people talking and moving toward becoming a paying client.

Again, there are several ways to manage your inbound marketing strategy, but please, for the love of all that is good, do not rely on one source—that source could disappear at any time for any reason, so be prepared.

Here's what you need to do:

1. Join a networking group.
    a. Go online and find a group of people that is relevant to your industry and location; it will pay for itself if you put the right energy into it. You can do it!

2. Create an incentive program.
    a. People will work with you again and again if you give them a reason to come back.
    b. Create an offer or coupon for the *referral* customers.

3. Reward your constituents.
    a. Anyone who sends you business should get a piece of the pie or at least a pat on the back. Make sure that you never forget the people who helped you grow your business or achieve your goals; good *referral* partners are hard to come by!

Questions to Consider:

- *Why would I want a referral instead of someone from the internet, a cold call, or walking into my store?*
    - Referrals are much more likely to start paying you, stay with you, and also are more likely to be aligned with your *values* (see Value), so they're much easier to work with overall.

- *What if my clients' privacy is extremely important, so referrals are extremely difficult to obtain?*
  - Every client's privacy is important, so treat their personal data as if it were your own, and they will respect you, thus, giving you a better chance at receiving *referrals*.

Troubleshooting

- If you're having trouble getting *referrals*, don't worry; all you need to do is showcase your existing products or services so that people want to work with you. If you think you work in a boring industry, lean into it. Showcase the "boring" elements of your industry and give the viewers the opportunity to get to know you and your business—even the ugly parts. Remember, there is no replacement for the truth.

Story

When I first started my business, I was under the impression that I needed to make three hundred cold calls a day to get new clients. As fate would have it, this was not true (although it is a viable strategy for some people). In my opinion, if you have to make three hundred cold calls a day to get new clients, you haven't spent enough time perfecting your product or service. People should want to work with you without you having to persuade them—a.k.a. *referrals*.

After realizing that making three hundred cold calls a day wasn't my cup of tea, I started looking for new ways to get clients. It turns out, all you have to do is meet one new person every single day. Even if it's on the phone, over the internet, or in person, go out of your way to meet at least one new person every day, and your network will become as vast as you want it to be, thus, increasing your chances of getting *referrals* and increasing your revenue.

Story

Every business and every business owner has a story but has it been written out to that it can be easily understood by your target audience? Is it relatable? Does it create a gravity toward your company and your staff for clients and potential customers to relate to you and become customers for life? It's okay to hire a professional to help you write your *story*, but the original *story* needs to come from you, the business owner; otherwise, it will just be a translation of the actual events of the timeline of the business and can come off as dry or insincere.

After you have written your story, ask your employees to tell their stories and add those stories to your website and other publications about your business. When you have a clearly *illustrated* story that's prominent on your website and social media platforms, it allows outsiders (potential clients) to easily make a decision about working with you. Whether it's prospective clients or existing employees, viewers can get an inside look at your business and can, therefore, make a clear decision on what they think of you and your team; the easier it is for viewers to make a decision about you, the more they will trust you and your business.

So many times, I see businesses and business owners focusing on what their business does—the literals. Instead, talk about client success *stories*, employee success *stories*, and your company's *story* so that people can relate to you and your business. This makes them more at ease with starting work with you or buying from you for the rest of their lives.

Here's what you need to do:

1. Write the story of yourself and your business.
   a. Easier said than done; I know. Believe it or not, people do care about your story, even if all you're doing is setting up chairs, tents, and tables; people want to know who they're working with; give them a piece of your personality!
      i. No one wants to write their story, but it gives the target audience an idea of who, what, why, and where they're working with.

Questions to Consider:

- *What if my business is extremely straightforward, and we provide a service that doesn't need a story?*
   - From my experience, every business is different, and maybe you're right; your business is so straightforward that you don't need a story. Well, I can tell you for certain that if you did apply a *story* to your business, you will *gather* (see Gather) a stronger following and, therefore, increase revenue.

- *Should I mention other peoples' stories within my brand's (see Brand) story?*
   - Absolutely (see Illuminate)!

Troubleshooting

1. Make sure your story is
   a. authentic,
      i. Customers will know right away when a brand is being inauthentic, disingenuous, or careless.

    b.   differentiated, and
- i. Personality, innovation, or design can either make you stand out or fade in.

    c.   consistent.
- i. Recognition and familiarity are powerful. Commit your brand to your audience's memory.

Story

    Here I am writing a story about a *story;* if that's not ironic enough for you, then I don't know what is; let's get to it. Everyone has a *story*; some people's stories are more engaging than others, but not for the reasons you might think. For example, everyone graduated high school (or at least we hope so). At face value, that sounds like a really boring story. However, if you talk about the fact that you went to the best high school in your hometown, skipped class, went to prom, and learned a life lesson along the way, the *story* suddenly becomes a lot more interesting.

    I like to compare this to the way most people will tell you, "I'm not creative" or "my life isn't interesting;" no one's life is interesting. It's all about how you present the information and tell the *story*. You could be one out of ten people selling ice cream in a single square mile radius, but if you talk about how you made your way from selling snow cones to ice cream and talk about each step you took to grow your business, you'll find that people are suddenly a *lot* more interested in what you're saying.

Truth

Nothing beats the truth when talking about public relations and marketing strategies. If an employee, a company, or a business owner makes a mistake, that person should own it publicly and state your proposed solution to the problem as soon as possible (after formulating a response plan with your team so that everyone is in agreement on the *messaging*). This gives credibility to the business and positions you and your team as leaders in your industry; people want the *truth*, so don't withhold it, especially when you know it.

When telling the *truth*, you will likely get a full spectrum of reactions from people within your audience. It's important to take the negative comments with a grain of salt and run with the positivity that others provide you as much as possible.

Whether we're talking about a marketing campaign, a new software implementation, or a training session for new employees, make sure you're telling your employees and customers the *truth*. You may have heard of the phrase "truth in advertising" before it's because there are so many companies that *don't* tell the *truth* when it could have really helped them. You have probably seen countless CEOs, politicians, and companies as a whole fumble public relations situations by giving roundabout answers to questions or by presenting a partial *truth*, which in employees' and customers' eyes is the same if not worse than directly lying.

Bad things happen to good people, and bad things happen to good businesses; every business goes through ups and downs. The best thing a business can do when something bad *does* happen is to get in front of the *story* before the media inevitably discovers the *truth* and fabricates their own interpretation (which can harm your business).

The same goes when talking to your employees; for example, if you're having cash flow issues and will have to pay your staff late, use this an opportunity to buy yourself some goodwill by telling them the *truth*. Additionally, if you mess up a customer's product or service, own the mistake and let the customer know that you are actively working on a solution. If you wait until they find out on their own, you have no control over what is said, and that's bad for business.

Here's what you need to do:

1. Talk to your employees and get to know them; don't be afraid to ask questions and have fun.
    a. Getting to know your employees' *truths* is a win-win. When you and your team are on the same page, anything is possible—so stick with the *truth*.

2. Create a crisis plan.
    a. This doesn't sound like fun; that's because it isn't. However, having a public relations crisis plan can save your company from severe damage to public perception if it's created and executed correctly.
    b. Your crisis plan should function like a fire drill. Everyone on your staff should know the exact process in the event of a public relations crisis, just the same as they should know where the fire exits are in the building.

Questions to Consider:

- *What if the truth will make me lose a client, employee, or even my entire business?*
    o If this is the case for you or your business, you should strongly consider a rebrand and also a reassessment of your goals and aspirations because if your *truth* will get you killed, you should lead a different life.

- *Is there ever a time in which the truth isn't the best option for my business's well-being?*
    - Nope—the only time that it's even somewhat of a plausible option is if you are honest with the client or customer about your inability to do something and then you tell them you will figure it out (assuming you promised you could do something and couldn't), but even in this instance, you're still telling the truth, so the answer remains no *(do not see no—this is a hard "no," so there's no need to look for further explanation).*

Troubleshooting

- If you're having doubts about whether or not you or your company has been truthful in all situations, have someone scan through your social media accounts, client communications, and screen phone calls once a month; this will pay dividends in the long run.
    - If you discover something that should be corrected, correct it. Every situation is different, but if you know the difference between right and wrong, you'll know how to correct the issue.

Story

If you take one thing away from this book, it's that there is no substitute for the *truth*. This is the first thing that you learn in any public relations class, and it's not by mistake that they teach you this. There are a multitude of examples of companies trying to cover up their mistakes rather than taking ownership of their problems, and it always ends in disaster, and the public always finds out anyway, so stick with the *truth*.

THE ADVERTISER'S ALPHABET

Unless your goal is to be the laughing stock of whatever the most current issue is, you should always precede the press, your employees, your business, and even yourself (see You) with the *truth*. Cover ups can be a slippery slope into a false reality, so tread carefully; the *truth* is always the best option; however good or bad it may be—people will respect you for it.

Umbrella

Create a data *umbrella* to protect yourself and your company from unpredictable and unforeseen forces. *Collecting data on a regular basis and implementing a data umbrella will save you and your business from hours of backtracking and retracing steps to find solutions to simple problems.* When you make data-driven decisions, you're decreasing your chances of failure and improving your chances of success. There are no absolutes or guarantees in marketing; I consider my job to be risk-mitigating because if you're doing it right, paid advertising is much like counting cards in blackjack; *you can improve your chances of success, but there will always be statistics involved.*

Making a data *umbrella* sounds more difficult than it is; if you have customer-relationship management software, you're ahead of the game. If not, pen and paper or an Excel Spreadsheet is a great place to start. Ideally, you want to be collecting demographic and psychographic data as much as possible. This means that you want to be notating customers' ages, locations, genders, behaviors, and interests into a document so that you can take averages of those numbers and data points and turn them into a clear-cut target audience profile. Data saves lives!

When you apply your data to your marketing campaign, marketing becomes one of the easiest things you've ever done to grow your business. You no longer have doubts or questions in the back of your mind about why you're running an ad; it makes sense to do run an ad to a specific group of people at a specific time because the data confirm it; you'll lose a lot less sleep, trust me.

Google Analytics (GA), Google Search Console (GSC), and your Google My Business (Profile) (GMB) Listing accounts are key tools that I use to measure client success. Don't let all the buttons intimidate you into doing nothing with these tools because when used correctly, you may not even have to spend money on ads to get clients.

Another place to collect and implement data is through email and SMS marketing platforms such as Mailchimp, HubSpot, or Marketing 360. *An interesting tidbit for you:* the people that like and engage with your content are not always the same people that will pay for your products or services. For my business, the audiences are completely different from one another; this means that growing my following and getting new clients require two completely separate marketing strategies.

    The real fun begins once you've been collecting data for at least thirteen months (that's not a typo). At thirteen months of data, you will have the ability to start comparing year over year, monthly data sets. For instance, I could be looking at key word data from Google Search Console and Google My Business from January of last year while comparing it to January of this year. If the key words used to find your website and listing are exactly the same as last year (with an increase in number of clicks for those keywords), you know that you have made a year over year improvement in online visibility. Take it a step further, and compare these key words to the key words found through a platform like Yoast (an SEO tool), and if those key words match in all four places (GA, GSC, GMB, Yoast), then I think you would agree with me if I told you that the data was extremely accurate and could be used for paid advertising target audience acquisition (sales in short).

    Of course, there is always the possibility (and probability) that you have conflicting data sets. Don't fret; this just means that you need to categorically equalize your platforms' (website, GMB, Yoast, social media content, etc.) key words so that no matter where your potential client or customer views your business, they are getting the exact same experience on all platforms. In turn, this will make the search engine algorithms treat your website much better when it comes to displaying search results; it's a win-win; it just takes some work.

    In short, when you create your data umbrella, you create your revenue *umbrella*.

Here's what you need to do:

1. Make sure you have the full gamut of Google tools set up and easily accessible at all times.
    a. This includes Google Analytics, Google Search Console, Google Tag Manager, Google My Business, and, preferably, Google Workspace (includes your company email and Google Drive [storage]).

2. Make sure that you have someone (who understands the platforms) monitoring these tools at least once a month; once per week is best, and daily usage and monitoring are where you can make some real money.

Questions to Consider:

- *What if I am a solopreneur and I don't need protection or I have people do it for me?*
    - It's actually best to have professionals do this for you, but please, for the love of all that is good, make sure that you are aware of how these protections function, so in the event of their failure, you are able to recover promptly and with finesse.

- *How can I make my umbrella more reliable?*
    - The simplest answer is to collect more data on previous or existing clients. The more data and data sets you have, the more accurate and reliable the information will be.
    - Alternatively, you can make your *umbrella* more reliable by educating your employees so that they can help create and sustain the *umbrella* for you (see Gather).

Troubleshooting

- If you don't have any existing data or Google accounts set up, that's okay. Have a professional help you set them up as soon as possible. Every you're not collectin' data is considered a day of data lost.
- When you don't have data, it's extremely important to make the client demographics and psychographics document mentioned in this section. Unless you're a start-up on day one, there is always some type of data you can retroactively collect to improve your business.

Story

Preparing for the rain by having an *umbrella* seems like an easy task, right? Once you take into consideration the part where you have to first, remember to add an *umbrella* to your shopping list, go to the store, find the aisle where the *umbrellas* are, wait in line, get in the car, make it home, and then, more importantly, remember to put it next to the door so that you actually use it when a storm is coming; you start to realize that there's a lot more that goes into staying dry than you think.

That all may seem like hearsay, but the point is that it has not been easy for me to set up an *umbrella* for my company, my employees, and myself, but it's important to have one, so I persevered. Do whatever it takes to secure, protect, and solidify your ideas, your business, and your employees because, unfortunately, there are a *lot* of people out there looking to take advantage of you and use you for your ideas (and much more). This may be my own experience talking, but I have found this to be true time and time again, especially within higher levels of management.

For instance, I was selling a product my team and I made to a company, and the deal was set to go through upward of seven figures until, all of a sudden, they weren't interested; I'd bet my life savings they took the idea and will recreate it on their own dime, and there isn't much that can be done, except to learn from that experience.

So long story short, make sure you spend time crafting and perfecting the *umbrella* (in my case, a stronger NDA with more severe repercussions) for your assets, whether they're people or ideas.

Value

Creating value and perceiving value by carefully crafting and packaging your products and services into items that your target audience can easily understand and relate to; a potential customer that knows exactly what they are about to buy is much more likely to convert than someone who is confused by your offer. Perceived value is when you see something that is marked down from $997 to $97; most people will know this is a load of shit, but that's what it is; you want to stay away from such extremes, but I wanted to get my point across. And always make sure that the perceived *value* in your *messaging* strategy is worth boasting because once you tell someone that you're selling something for 10 percent of its *value*, you'll no longer be taken seriously.

Instead of telling customers how much money they're saving by working with you, *teach* them about how their results relate to their return on investment *(by the way, I pondered making the letter T "teach" instead of "truth" for quite some time because of how important educating your customers is to your success).* Anyways, return on investment (ROI) doesn't always mean money. If you're in health care, for example, your customers' return on investment is their bettered health. As a continuation of the healthcare example, if you're a chiropractor, you should be teaching your clients about why you're making the adjustments you're giving them; this will reduce (if not eliminate) the common problem of clients coming in and asking for specific adjustments that don't align with their overall care plan.

Do not try and trick or persuade people into buying from you; this will only create dissociation from you, your *brand*, and your product or service. Those people will (inevitably) spread the *truth* (see Truth) about your methodology, and it will hurt your business's public perception. Instead, spread educational video content and blog posts that build *value* around you, your *brand*, business, and staff so that potential clients and customers feel cared for when working with or buying from you. Give customers a top-notch experience that they can remember and value for years to come so that you can grow your business. Creating and perceiving value also spurs *referrals* (see Referrals).

Value and perceived *value* are what serves as a primary attention grabber when you're trying to convince someone (who hasn't heard about you, your product, or your service) to buy from you.

Here's what you need to do:

1. Create an offer.
    a. What are you selling, how much are you selling it for, and how long is the offer valid? Make these things clear to your target audience.

2. Compare your offer to your competitive landscape. What are competitors in your area offering and is it a better option than what you're offering?

3. Record data during a closed-ended time period so that you can later analyze results and compare them to a new offer next month or, ideally, the same offer from last year (during the same time period).
    a. These things will become systematic over time; starting is always the hardest part.

Questions to Consider:

- *What if I don't know how to value my products and services; what do I do?*
    - This is a common problem, especially if you're in the service industry. If you can't find someone in your industry to compare your pricing to, then you'll need to get creative and possibly hire a professional.

- *What if my employees disagree with me about the value I place on my products and services?*
    - When (not if) this happens, you need to tell them the *truth* (see Truth) about your financials so that they understand why you are charging what you're charging and where the money goes. Explain to them that you charge what you charge to provide an exceptional level of quality service that can't be found anywhere else.
        - Alternatively (this isn't my taste, but I've seen it work), you can say that you charge as little as you do and provide as little service as you do, and you're the cheapest on the market.

Troubleshooting

- When people inevitably give you shit about your offer, ad, or *messaging*, don't change course; this can almost always be chalked up to "the cost of doing business." However, if you carefully contour your *messaging*, offer, and ad, you will see a reduced number of complaints and negative comments and an increased number of positive affirmations.
    - Remember, run with the positivity and ignore the negativity as much as possible.
- Don't under*value* yourself just because people aren't interested in a brand-new product or service. If the people commenting on your new product or service can't afford it, let them be and continue working on your target audience; you may just have a target audience that is hard to reach, but there's always a way to get to them!

Story

Value-adds, as they're called, can come in many different forms. When I had a potential client on the fence about working with me, I told them I'd fly there to meet them in person, and this *accommodation* tactic (actually) failed, but I now have them as a reference and contact for future work because I put my value before my services (their payment).

People want service before *value*, and you can easily give it to them if you know your clients' needs, wants, and interests, so don't be shy and don't hold back on giving potential clients information you've worked hard to obtain because if they don't get it from you, they'll get it from someone else.

Wait

Wait and actively listen to what your clients, customers, and employees are telling you; believe it or not, they're real people (just like you), and they want their voices heard and responded to in an individualized manner. WAIT is a useful acronym that I recently came across during a networking meeting; it stands for "Why am I talking?" This may sound silly, but when it comes to your *messaging* strategy or an important sales call, waiting before speaking can mean the difference in wasted time and making money. Instead of proactively telling your potential client about your services (most businesses do this), try waiting, listening, and then asking strategic questions that guide the conversation toward a solution that you provide if it's a good fit.

When you focus on listening to your potential client and taking notes on their wants and needs, you can be much more efficient with your strategic questioning. When you are asking relevant, strategic questions, you position yourself as an authority in the conversation and as a professional in your industry. Once you've positioned yourself as an authority (whether it be during a conversation or during a multimillion-dollar campaign), the potential customer no longer has any need to think about your competitors, which makes the sales process much easier for you.

Make sure that every word and phrase you use on sales calls or during client interactions are moving you closer to the sale. Try to avoid going off on tangents and stick to strategic questions and information (rather than persuasion and manipulation). When you inform the potential buyer about the results and positive outcomes of your product or service, and they are still not sold, then your product or service isn't a good fit for them; I'd suggest moving onto someone else. Don't turn the informative conversation into an argument. If the potential customer is a good fit, wrap up the call and give them action items for the next call.

Waiting also applies to digital marketing campaigns. When you're running content through the algorithms (posting on social media) across Facebook, Instagram, LinkedIn, Google My Business, and any other digital platform, make sure that you are on a consistent schedule. Yes, it's good to post "more often," but treat these platforms' guidelines as attendance policies or credit scores: don't be late, don't be early, and make sure the content is as high-quality as possible. For example, it's better to have one high-quality post on Friday mornings at 10 a.m. than it is to have two posts that are done in the middle of the night during the same week.

You can always increase your baseline level of activity (how often you post), but decreasing your activity level (becoming inconsistent) tells the algorithms that your business is in decline, and your cost per impression will skyrocket. Even if you're not running paid ads, you don't want a high cost per impression, so *wait* and perfect your content before posting at the right time.

Here's what you need to do:

1. Practice *waiting* and responding to potential clients, customers, and employees during every interaction, and you will find that it becomes easier.

2. Create a schedule for your social media posts.
    a. You want to know what day, time, and wording will be used before making a post so that it can be edited if needed.

3. Make a list of strategic questions that can be used by you and your staff when talking to customers about your product or service.
    a. Ask the potential customers questions that relate to what you're selling so that your product or service surfaces naturally as a solution to their problem.

Questions to Consider:

- *Why am I talking (WAIT)?*
    - This is one of my favorite acronyms when it comes to sales strategies. If what you're saying to an employee or client isn't moving you and your team closer to your goal, what are you saying and why (sorry to answer a question with a question, but it's true)?

- *What if I don't have time to wait? (I have bills to pay, Andrew, what are you talking about?)*
    - If you're in this position, get a second or third job; don't risk your business's integrity and *brand* (see Brand) over a utility bill or car payment; it's not worth it in the long run, and it will get you in trouble.

Troubleshooting

- If you're having trouble waiting inside of conversations, try learning more about your product service or industry so that there is nothing someone can ask you that would intimidate you. I've found that it is usually a lack of knowledge about the product or service that makes sales teams lean more toward running through their script or demo instead of treating the client like a human being and answering relevant questions.

Story

Waiting is one of the hardest things to do as a business owner, especially if you have payroll to make, deadlines to meet, or bills to pay. However, if you want the most money for your product or service and want to extract every dollar from your hard work, sometimes *waiting* is the best way to make a sale. For instance, it took me over a year to close one of my highest-paying clients. I spent months and months trying to get them on a phone call (via numerous emails), but when I finally had them on a call, it was an easy close because I waited for the right moment and when they were ready; I wasn't pushy or desperate with them; I *waited*.

It's not about when you are ready to make the close, it's about when the potential client or customer is ready to buy, and you, the seller, need to be perceptive of when the buyer is ready. Do not rush anyone into anything; stick to information and education rather than pushing and persuading.

X Variable

Use the x factor to create a winning equation. *With every marketing strategy, there is a multitude of variables that can lead to failure; I consider my job to be risk-mitigating for this reason.* Key examples of variables are target audience traits, *brand* voice, *brand* personality, timeline, estimated return on investment, creative strategy, and budget. It's easy to get excited about marketing and end up spending months and thousands of dollars without making any progress; this is why it's important to narrow your vision and focus on a singular goal to start. Once you achieve your first goal, you can add more goals (variables) to the equation and in turn, more revenue. For example, if you're a dine-in restaurant, the first goal you want functional is your reservations. Once those are working, you can add online ordering. Once you've added online ordering, then you can add delivery. Master one process at a time instead of trying to jump into everything at once.

So what's the first variable you should tackle? It depends on your business. Let's say you want more phone calls from people interested in your product or service; you'll want to set up a conversion goal for phone calls from your Google Ads that simplifies the first variable. You'll then want to make sure you're recording those phone calls so that you can audit them and provide training to your employees—online payments or scheduling should be added as well. Once you have the systems in place that allow you to properly handle the existing amount of phone calls, you can start thinking about a paid, digital campaign to get *more* calls without worrying about whether or not there will be someone to answer the phone (pay attention to your flight schedule [paid advertising runtime schedule] so that people aren't calling you outside business hours).

When you systematically add more variables to your equation, you'll find that it's much easier to scale your business in increments than it is when you've just launched a new campaign with three new variables. So whether you want more online purchases, more people visiting your location, more phone calls, more awareness, or a combination of a few, pick a problem to solve and stick with it until you've created a tracking system around it. Tracking and measurement are fundamental to success, and you can't track or measure problems you can't see (or solve for), so take the time to find and implement the right processes for you and your staff to grow your business. In other words, don't try doing long division with pencil and paper if there's a calculator nearby; check your resources first and formulate a growth plan that fits your needs.

Here's what you need to do:

1. Create a list of existing variables in your business, as well as variables that can appear in the future.
    a. Some Examples
        i. *Target Audience Traits*
            1. Age, gender, location, behaviors, and interests.
        ii. *Brand Voice*
            1. What should your *brand* sound like during *messaging* (serious, playful, or logical)?
        iii. *Brand Personality*
            1. What are adjectives that describe your business and *brand*?
        iv. *Timeline*
            1. Write the major events of the business in chronological order so others can understand if needed.
2. What is the timeframe on your campaign and investment strategy? Is it open-ended or close-ended? Weekdays and weekends, or just weekends?

THE ADVERTISER'S ALPHABET

3. What is the average amount of time someone works with you? This is used to calculate the second half of average lifetime customer value (LCV).
    a. *Average lifetime customer value is the average number of dollars someone spends with you divided by the average amount of time they spend with you.*
        i. Estimated Return on Investment
            1. How much money are you expecting to gross and profit on your investment?
        ii. *Creative Strategy*
            1. What channels and mediums are used to showcase your product or service during the campaign's timeframe? Are you using strictly-digital tactics, or are you also using TV and radio?
        iii. *Budget/Investment*
            1. What's the total monthly, weekly, daily, and so forth budget(s) for the time spent on advertising? Please never lose sight of this.

4. How much are you willing to spend on the growth of your business?

5. How much are you willing to lose on your marketing strategy? It's easy to talk about how much you can *make*, but how much can you afford to *lose*?
    a. People will argue with me about this, but for some businesses, marketing is the last thing you should be worried about if you don't have your internal operations detailed and understood by you and your entire team. It's completely fine to be in this

situation, but don't make a bad situation worse by exacerbating issues caused by operational inefficiencies.

6. Implement systems and processes to automate what you can without depersonalizing your sales process; people want to be remembered!
    a. Online Scheduling
    b. Phone Call Recording
    c. Review Management

Questions to Consider:

- *There are so many variables; I don't know where to start. How do I simplify my strategy into something that I can understand?*
    - Pretend your business was started yesterday; what's the first thing you would do? Ideally, it would be an assessment of your target market and structuring of your brand, but it can be anything from creating a budget and timeline to fine-tuning your audience on Google Ads.

- *My business doesn't change, so variables don't affect me; do I need to worry about this?*
    - Even if you decide to make no choice at all, you are still making a choice. In this case, you'd be ignoring data that could potentially make or break your business; for the sake of your business, your family, and your employees, please don't ignore variables and change. I'm sure you've heard the saying, "The only constant is change," and it's true, so prepare for it by implementing systems and processes that streamline your business.

Troubleshooting

- You're going to run into issues when implementing new systems and processes for your business; there's no way around it. This is where careful planning and procedure will help you get more sleep at night.
- It usually takes at least one month for small or medium-sized businesses to implement a new process, so take the time to outline the changes to your staff to prevent miscommunications and missteps.
- Remember, the entire idea of this section is to decrease the number of problems you have into an equation you can solve for, so do your best to stay high-level when approaching these issues. It's easy to get caught up on why the scheduling system is broken or why one of your employees missed a phone call. You're the business owner, so focus on moving your entire business forward rather than trying to move the scheduling system forward; hire someone to do that.

Story

We've all heard the saying, "The only constant is change," and it's true, and that's why I've chosen X to signify *variable* change. For example, for the first year that I was in business, my business model changed at least once per month, if not more often, and that's okay. As a business owner, one of the most important things you can do for the success of your business is embrace change. When the COVID-19 shutdown hit in March 2020, I had roughly forty-five clients I was working with at the time, and looking back, it's easy to see the difference between the business owners who closed their doors permanently and the business owners who closed their doors temporarily because of state restrictions.

It had nothing to do with intelligence, grit, or any of the other traits you might guess would equate to operating a successful brick-

and-mortar location during the COVID-19 crisis. *The only difference between those who succeeded, excelled, and overcame the economic downturn caused by the pandemic was the business owners' willingness to adapt to the changing circumstances.* Believe it or not, that's all it was.

For instance, my clients in the healthcare field (let's use chiropractors as an example) were faced with an odd challenge; in some states, their business was not considered "essential," so they were left with two options:

1. Close their doors and wait until the governor in their state allowed them to reopen or deemed them an essential business.
2. Find a way to monetize the opportunity presented to them by COVID-19.

The business owners who chose option two actually grew their businesses whilst their competitors' businesses were in a steady decline or shut down completely.

I use the word opportunity instead of crisis because, especially as a business owner, you need to view everything as an opportunity for growth and change, no matter how bad or good the situation is.

You

Put yourself front and center. This your business, your life, and your plan, so *you* are the one that needs to make the final decision. *You can teach people about your business, and you can pay people to learn about and work for your business, but their work will always be a translation of your thoughts and ideas.*

There are several ways to mitigate the effect that these translations have on your business that should be employed. The length of time someone has been working for you is one of the biggest factors that I've seen become a detriment to a business's success. It's great to have someone that knows your processes inside and out but don't let them take *you* off your path and original plan for your business unless you've paid them to give you advice about a change. If you create a rock-solid training program for your employees, there should be no question about how something should be completed, and this makes fewer miscommunications and opportunities for failure. Create a system where your employees do the work, and then you, the decision-maker, can come and check the work as quality control. Another way to mitigate damage caused by idea-translation is to have morning meetings that outline the plan for the day—make the plan easy to understand, and use this time to motivate your employees and answer many common questions from your staff.

Take ownership for all the successes, failures, and shortcomings that are associated with your business; you are the leader, so do not place blame on others for the failure of your strategy. When you take ownership for the failures and give credit to your employees for the successes, you position yourself as a leader worth following. Taking ownership means that you should visibly own your mistakes in front of your employees and customers to create an example of leadership that *you* want within your company. If something isn't working, yes, it might be someone else's fault, but it's your job as a leader to take the blame (not distribute it) and teach your employees how to handle similar situations for future reference. For instance, if a customer walks into your store saying that they had a bad experience, acknowledge and apologize for the situation while working to find a solution. You can meet with your employees later to discuss what happened, but always take care of the customer first.

Here's what you need to do:

1. Create a training program for incoming employees.
    a. Make sure there's a page by page set of instructions for every new employee that outlines their specific job duties so that they know if they're properly progressing through your company.
    b. Allow your employees to make edits and suggestions to this document based on their experiences.

2. Create an onboarding or introductory program for new clients or customers.
    a. Your clients and customers don't know how your business functions, so make sure that they understand what they're supposed to be doing to work with you. I've seen businesses lose clients before they ever had a chance to speak with them because their process wasn't well-defined.

3. Write the process or processes for customer relations so that your employees can take over in the event that you can't make it to work.
    a. If you didn't show up to work tomorrow, what would happen? Would everything function normally or, would the entire show come to an end?
    b. Make sure that your staff has access to every project and customer communication so they can take over if needed.

Questions to Consider:

- *What is this, a self-help book? Why is this part of a book on advertising?*
    - Before taking the first step on the journey of writing this book, I deliberated over it for weeks. "Is this a self-help book or a book on advertising?"
        - It's a book on advertising with some self-help mixed in. I'd apologize for it, but it's needed. As referenced earlier in the book, when a business owner (or anyone in a leadership position) is dealing with personal problems that are not being treated by professionals or handled properly, the people around them will feel the negativity, and it will bring the team and your company down.

- *Why is this book talking about me? Isn't this supposed to talk about how to help my business?*
    - As stated in the previous paragraph, if *you*, the business owner, are unwilling or unable to address your own emotions, thoughts, and actions from a larger perspective, in my opinion, your business is on borrowed time. From my experience, how much time *you* and your business have depends on the severity and amount of issues the owner or management is having.

Troubleshooting

- I spoke briefly about translations and how they affect your business. If there is any doubt in your mind that your employees' translations of your business and work aren't up to par, please address that as soon as possible because the damage they could be inflicting (on your behalf) is

almost always unknown because of the nature of client communications.
- It's okay (and completely normal) if this section brings up more problems than solutions for you; the good news is that there's always room for improvement, and if you're willing to do the work, then these issues won't affect you for long.

Story

Yep, we're talking about *you* this time. After working with hundreds of business owners, I can tell you with absolute certainty that any problems *you* are having in your personal life will directly reflect onto *your* work, whether *you're* a business owner or not. If *you* are a business owner, please, for the love of all that is good, do not subject *your* employees, customers, or clients to a uncalled-for "therapy" session at their expense. Instead, be proactive about your personal growth and handle it as a task separate from your work—very separate.

Additionally, it should be known that "monkeys see, monkeys do." In other words, your employees (and sometimes clients and customers) look up to *you* whether you realize it or not. It's important that you're setting the right example and that you act like the person you want to meet.

Zero

Every client, customer, or employee you lose moves you farther away from the number zero. It's impossible to retain every client and employee, but your mission should be to provide service and value at such a level that no one wants to leave. Yes, clients and employees leave for various reasons, but why did you start working with them in the first place? What was the original goal? Was it completed? Were there issues along the way? I have found that the single greatest tool to bring to the table in any relationship is education. If it's your employees, educate them on what made you successful as a business owner and help them see the path to their own success. Some employees want to be business owners, and some of them want to go home at 5 p.m. without having to worry about anything else. Both situations have educational opportunities for you, the business owner, to showcase your leadership skills and teach your staff how to be successful in their own way.

When we're talking about retaining clients, this strategy is completely dependent on your business model. If your selling clothes, client retention looks more like a fashion show than it does like follow-up phone calls for service-based industries. If you're in a doctor's office, client retention looks like five-star customer service coordinated with a consistent follow-up schedule. If you're in a restaurant, client retention is almost completely different in that it depends on whether your food tastes better than the guy across the street and if you treat your customers well when they visit you, no matter how they visit you (dine-in, takeout, or call for a reservation).

You only have one shot at a reputation as a business, so don't leave it to chance. Instead, be selective with who you start working with, whether they're a client or an employee. First, identify your own skill sets as a business owner and compare these to your job and task requirements. Once you do this, you will be able to easily see where you need to improve (or hire help); you streamline your business for efficiency and profitability by making sure everyone on your team has a vital role in the business. If someone's role isn't vital, create new tasks for them or help them find a new role at another company; people change jobs frequently these days.

Positioning yourself as a teacher rather than a salesperson creates the opportunity for a lifelong relationship that will benefit both you and the client, but sometimes it doesn't work out that way. In either case, stick to being the best version of yourself, and the right people will stick with you in the long run.

Here's what you need to do:

1. Make a list of clients you've lost.
    a. Call them and see what you can do to earn their business.
        i. If they don't want to work with you, find out what went wrong so that you can learn from the mistakes and improve your business.

2. Make a list of people who have left negative reviews (if you have any).
    a. Do your best to get in contact with these people and see what you can do to fix the situation.
        i. "Hey [customer name], I saw you left a negative review, and I wanted to see if there's anything I can do for you to give you a better perception of our company. I understand things didn't go well at the time of service, but I want you to know that my team and I are at your service until you feel as though you've been treated fairly. If we reach a fair conclusion, would you consider giving us a five-star review if you are satisfied with our service?"

3. Set up a plan for reputation management.
    a. If you're a company of more than fifty employees, reputation management can be a full-time job, and someone experienced in public relations should be handling these tasks for you.

Questions to Consider:

- *There's no way to retain every single client; how am I supposed to do this?*
    - You're right; the chances are slim to none that your business will be able to retain every single client you interact with, but I can guarantee you that you will see more success, less stress, and more reliability from your business if you treat every client (and employee) as if they're the last one you'll ever have because they very well might be.

- *Employees come and go; why would I spend time on this? It doesn't make any sense.*
    - There's no excuse to treat your customers and employees as anything other than extended family. Employees will undoubtedly make changes, but *you*, the business owner, should remain a beacon of reliability and consistency. When you do this and do it well, employees and customers won't want to leave.

Troubleshooting

- If you've lost clients for unjustifiable reasons, give them a call and see how you can fix the situation; ask them what you can do to make it right; you might be surprised how little it can take to *right* a wrong.

- I always get asked how to remove negative reviews on a Google My Business Profile or Yelp account. Let me be clear, if your intention and motive is to get the negative review removed rather than calling the past client or customer to actually resolve the issue, then you have bigger problems that I can't help you address.
  - I've also heard of previous employees leaving negative reviews for a business (acting as a customer) and the employer thinking the reviews are fake and should be removed—quite the contrary. If you are making people that want to work for you upset with your behavior, you should expect nothing less from the clients and customers you serve. The truth always comes out in the end, so stick to what works, and stay true to yourself; the end result is much cleaner.

Story

Zero can be applied in a positive or negative manner to almost anything, but I want to stay on topic, so let's stay positive. If you're a business owner, you should know that it's quite a bit cheaper to maintain an existing client than it is to acquire a new client. The number *zero* is important because it's the number of clients, customers, and employees that you want to avoid losing.

With every customer, client, or employee, there are time expenses, monetary expenses, and emotional expenses; I have seen employer after employer (either) fail to see or ignore these expenses at the (pun definitely intended) expense of the business owner and their business. Stop reaching for plus ones and start hanging onto zeroes; it's much better for your health and your business. In other words, take care of what you have instead of trying to always cash grab and take what you can.

A Little Extra

I want to speak as frankly as possible in this section; life's too short to "wish I would've said something."

If you are a business owner, a manager, or a leader of any kind, please make sure you are properly paying and taking good care of your employees, contractors, and customers because you wouldn't be in business without them; don't take them for granted.

If you died tomorrow, would you be proud of what you've accomplished in life? If not, it's okay; it's never too late to start living the life you've always wanted. All you have to do is take a single step in the right direction while taking life one day at a time. Remember, most overnight successes take years, so get started now; you can do it!

About the Author

Andrew Hindle started his entrepreneurial career mowing lawns when he was twelve years old by printing flyers and placing them in his neighbor's mailbox. Since then, he has been nominated for artwork awards during high school; he has owned a computer repair business during his college career and became a professional music producer while living in New York City.

Andrew is the author of a comedy page on Facebook, "The Geriatric Kid," and owns and operates a clothing company, Icon Army. He graduated from Texas Tech University (with honors) with a degree in mass communications, specializing in advertising. During his college career, he was a member of a couple of elite advertising teams, two of which created advertising campaigns for Charles Schwab and Wienerschnitzel, the hot dog fast-food chain.

He also coauthored two dissertations specializing in target audience research, analysis, and acquisition, where he learned how to turn data into money. After working at two agencies (one being the largest in the state), he now focuses the majority of his time on his primary company, Stacked Deck, where every client gets a unique battle plan for their business and hasn't looked back since. His mission is to overturn the negative dogma surrounding advertising so that clients around the world can believe that advertising work can be done honestly and at high quality.

Printed in the USA
CPSIA information can be obtained
at www.ICGtesting.com
LVHW091217081024
793245LV00002B/318

9 798885 058087